Be Sharp

"Tell Me About Yourself" in
Great Introductions and Professional Bios

SECOND EDITION

PAULA ASINOF & MINA BROWN

Be Sharp: "Tell Me About Yourself" in Great Introductions and Professional Bios
Second Edition

Copyright © 2018 Paula Asinof and Mina Brown.

All rights reserved. No part of this book may be reproduced in whole or in part without the written permission from the authors.

First Edition: December 2008

ISBN-13: 978-1975717261
ISBN-10: 1975717260

DEDICATION

To our loyal customers, clients, and colleagues
who have successfully implemented our approach and
spread the word about the power and benefits of a
polished personal introduction and well-honed bio.

Paula & Mina

TABLE OF CONTENTS

Introduction vii

PART ONE: PERSONAL INTRODUCTIONS
Chapter 1   Introductions Need Power and Pizzazz 3
Chapter 2   Why Is This So Hard? 7
Chapter 3   Recipe for a Polished Introduction 11
Chapter 4   Your Essence Factor 15
Chapter 5   Your Guru Factor 19
Chapter 6   Your Star Factor 23
Chapter 7   Putting it All Together 29
Chapter 8   Your Intro is a Gateway 35

PART TWO: PROFESSIONAL BIOS
Chapter 9   Why Do I Need a Bio? 41
Chapter 10   Why Most Bios Are Bad 49
Chapter 11   The Foundation Bio 51

PART THREE: BEYOND THE BASIC BIO
Chapter 12   Variety of Bios and Applications 81
Chapter 13   Bios for Job Search 85
Chapter 14   Your Web Presence 89
Chapter 15   Profiles 95
Chapter 16   Bios for Marketing 101
Chapter 17   Bios for Public Speaking 105
Chapter 18   Bios for Prospective Board Members 109

Conclusion 117
About the Authors 119

INTRODUCTION

Since the first edition of this book was published in 2008, the world has changed—there are more models of recruiting, styles of interviewing, expanded talent development practices, and movement to a "gig" economy. You have more opportunities and requirements than ever to introduce yourself to different audiences. Whether you are looking for a job, angling for an internal promotion, starting your own business, looking for investors, or seeking contract opportunities, the power of a good personal introduction makes a world of difference.

> Barbara Corcoran (@BarbaraCorcoran), a New York City real estate mogul, Shark Tank Shark, and former Dancing with the Stars contestant, tweeted **"My favorite question—tell me a little bit about yourself."** 7 January 2018, 9:04 pm. She tweeted this live during the Shark Tank episode in which she made a deal with an entrepreneur who knew exactly how to answer this question for Barbara.

The principles presented in the First Edition have firmly stood the test of time. Our readers and clients continue to affirm the value of applying these approaches in their individual endeavors. Now with technology advances, accelerating change, and continuing globalization of business, executing on these principles demands more agility, sophistication, and flexibility. We have built on the original content to address applications and nuances that didn't exist when we first wrote the book and eliminated some applications that are no longer relevant. In addition, we have incorporated the feedback and suggestions our readers have shared.

We have continued to develop our methodology and easy-to-use tools that can help anyone develop their own unique introduction. It is an easy step from there to writing a professional bio, a compelling resume, and other profiles. By helping you understand the importance of "Tell me about yourself," we hope to empower you in all your business and personal interactions.

A LOOK INSIDE

Part One. Personal Introductions. Learn how to respond to "Tell me about yourself" with confidence and polish. It's not obvious to most people how to do this, so we have created an easy formula for nailing this every time in every situation. Preparation and practice are key.

Part Two. Professional Bios. Most professionals should have something like a professional bio that tells their story in a concise and targeted way. The bio needs to be engaging and attractive. You are presenting who you are along with your entire career in one easy-to-read page. We walk you through the process from top to bottom. Highlighting what's important to your audience is essential.

Part Three. Beyond the Basic Bio. A bio is not a bio is not a bio. There are numerous situations where you need a bio or similar document that is uniquely constructed. This section presents several of the most common business circumstances where a special layout is needed. For each situation, you will learn how to take your Foundation Bio and create an appropriate customized version.

Once you have created your introduction and bio, you will find that they take on a life of their own. Applications range from presenting yourself on the web, marketing your business, and applying for Board consideration. This section provides specific guidance for these situations.

Part One

PERSONAL INTRODUCTIONS

Chapter 1

INTRODUCTIONS NEED POWER AND PIZZAZZ

Every time you meet someone—or present yourself for the first time—you are creating an impression so lasting that good or bad, it can be difficult to change. In today's fast moving and relentless business environment, these opportunities occur almost every day. It may be the new boss, the new client, or the job candidate you've been asked to interview. You may be invited to present an award or speak to a conference. Or you may be meeting a potential boss as part of the job interview process. A strong positive impression can result in a job offer, a new client contract, or better business relations. A bad first impression can make others doubt your abilities, mistrust your motives, or see you as a liability. As Susan Bixler, a pioneering coach in the field of professional image, points out, "Although people should be judged by their innate worth, it is often a first impression that determines whether someone will stick around long enough to let them reveal it."

Few people have the personality and self-confidence to pull off a flawless personal introduction without any advance preparation or thought. If you spend just a few minutes preparing to put your best foot forward, you can change the way the world sees you. You've probably heard the common wisdom "You never get a second chance to make a first impression."

PERSONAL INTRODUCTIONS

Even now, we rarely encounter people who initially respond to the request "Tell me about yourself" with professional polish and pizzazz. About half start by telling some version of their life story or recounting their resume. Others just ramble in a stream-of-consciousness sort of way. The rest appear to freeze—the "deer in headlights" look.

Yet this is one challenge that you will face over and over again. Our original research in the fall 2006 confirmed that "Tell me about yourself" was by far the most common interview question asked by recruiters. Since then, we continue to validate that this is a linchpin of interviews and other important situations where you need to make a good first impression. In a recent, hard-hitting article in Forbes, Liz Ryan, CEO & Founder of Human Workplace, wrote, "One question that still throws job seekers for a loop, is the question, 'So, tell me about yourself!'. . . . You've got to have something intelligent to say when you hear it. Often, it's the very first question you'll get as the interview begins." For example, the #1 sample question in the new video screening interview feature of a next generation applicant tracking system is..."Tell Us About Yourself."

Another interesting tidbit that shows how pervasive and ubiquitous this issue is comes from a simple Google search. The phrase "tell me about yourself" returns 33 million results, and the expanded phrase "tell me about yourself interview question" brings up 2 million links.

In particular, it is common practice for executive search consultants to start with "Would you tell me about yourself?" and then have the candidate spend the next one to two hours elaborating on their answer. These are expert interviewers who have learned that they can get the information they need by using the candidate's initial answer for follow-up questions.

As a general interviewing practice, there are a variety questions that are essentially the same as "Tell me about yourself." Even an opening question like, "What makes you a good candidate for this job?" should be answered with the ingredients of your personal introduction, maybe modified slightly to reflect the specific form of the question. Actually, whatever the first question is, you should try to frame your answer to incorporate elements of your personal introduction.

Here are other questions that are basically inviting you to start with your personal introduction and customize the response to the specific question.

- Tell me about your background.
- Why should we hire you?
- Summarize your experience.
- Give me the highlights of your career.
- Why don't you walk me through your job history?
- What expertise do you bring to the team?
- What do you feel are your best assets?
- Why are you interested in this job?

Candidates who fail to develop a polished and professional answer to that critical question are doing themselves a serious disservice. Still, this remains such a common deficiency among otherwise outstanding professionals that we decided to update this book with new examples and added guidance. More broadly than ever, a concise, well-honed personal introduction is needed in nearly all aspects of careers and business: job search, interviewing, LinkedIn profiles, networking, sales, marketing documents, websites, public speaking, teaching, publishing, internal promotion, new clients or teams, and more.

Clients who work with us on their introductions see firsthand the power of positive first impressions. We frequently hear that as a result of our training they can talk to people with new confidence, poise, and authority. For clients personally, many are surprised by new insights and perspectives that come from focusing on their unique and special qualities. Most people are uncomfortable and unclear about how to gracefully introduce themselves, and they are relieved to have an appropriate and meaningful way to do this—and it's a model they can use for a lifetime.

Chapter 2

WHY IS THIS SO HARD?

Despite the programs that train people to create their "30-second elevator pitch," most of what we hear today is just plain awful. These pitches are awkward, boring, irrelevant, too long, too short, cliché-ridden, stiff, rehearsed, and humorless. Once in a while, someone will introduce himself or herself the "right" way, and we remember that person. You probably do too.

You may think that honing a good introduction is simply a job interview skill, but what about meeting a new client, presenting yourself to a new team, or networking at industry events, community activities, and dinner parties. You may be an award nominee or honoree. Or you may be asked to be a guest speaker, to serve as a seminar leader, or to meet your boss's boss. And then there are situations like the first time you introduce yourself to your prospective in-laws. A good introduction is important any time you need to establish a connection with someone else quickly.

PERSONAL INTRODUCTIONS

What keeps *you* from introducing yourself with ease and confidence? Check all that apply. ☑

- ☐ It's impolite to brag.
- ☐ I don't know what to say.
- ☐ I'm embarrassed to talk about myself.
- ☐ I don't think I'm personally all that special.
- ☐ I'm afraid that people will judge me.
- ☐ No matter how much I prepare, I don't seem to be ready.
- ☐ I'm shy.
- ☐ It's too personal.
- ☐ I'm not confident enough to put myself in the spotlight.
- ☐ It's none of their business.
- ☐ I feel insincere.
- ☐ It feels superficial.
- ☐ The other person doesn't really want to know about me.
- ☐ I was brought up in a culture where it is inappropriate or rude for people to talk about themselves.

Cultural Bias

Every culture has its own view of what is considered polite. Most modern cultures, however, frown on people who talk continuously about their own accomplishments. While it is okay for someone else to describe you in glowing terms, it is generally considered impolite to say the same things about yourself. In this book, we will explain how you can talk deftly about yourself without appearing to brag.

Emotional Resistance

Fear of being judged is one of the most common reasons for poor personal introductions. People tend to be far more aware of their weaknesses than their strengths. Indeed, many people have such high expectations for themselves that they have a hard time focusing on what they do well. What if you were to ask someone else what your strengths or talents are? What would they say?

Learning how to pitch yourself is itself empowering. The very act of crafting your own introduction produces a sense of accomplishment and a higher level of self-esteem. Using our methodology, our clients often respond to their new introductions saying "Wow, is that really me? I like that person. I'd like to meet that person." Or even better, they say, "I'd like to interview that person."

Limiting Assumptions

We make assumptions every day, usually without stopping to think about their veracity. Often, these assumptions turn out to be self-defeating. When we are asked to describe ourselves, for example, it is easy to assume that people aren't really interested. We may think that they are just making conversation. Or we might assume that our answer will sound superficial or insincere. Done poorly, it actually may be superficial and insincere. Learning how to introduce yourself in any setting is an important statement about you. A good introduction must be not only factually accurate, but it must also come from the heart.

Lack of Skills

Most people would admit that they don't know how to properly respond to "Tell me about yourself". That's because most people have no model for developing a good introduction. No one has ever provided them with guidelines about what to say, what not to say, and how much information to provide.

For example, here are some common introduction mistakes. Have you ever heard (or said) any of these?

Life Chronology—This Is My Life: I was born in . . ., and raised in . . . . I went to college at. . . My first job was . . . I'm married and have two kids and two dogs.

Totally Personal Approach—All About Me: I'm very organized. I'm an early morning person, and my hobbies include bird watching, badminton, and video games.

PERSONAL INTRODUCTIONS

Just Jobs—Work Is My Life: I am the Vice President of . . . at . . . company. I am responsible for eight direct reports and an organization of 100 people. We manufacture widgets that are sold to . . . . I conduct weekly staff meetings at 8 a.m. on Mondays and quarterly all hands meetings. Prior to this job, I was the Director of . . . at . . . etc., etc., etc.

Inappropriate Information—Too Much Information (TMI): Oh there's so much to tell. Where do I start? I just moved into a new 3,000 square foot house and had so much trouble getting Internet service installed. I finally feel like I have my head above water, and I'm ready for work.

Answer with Question—So Help Me Out: What do you want to know?

Quizzical Look and Dead Silence—Duh.

This book will provide you with a simple, straightforward model for crafting an introduction that you can use effectively for the rest of your career and the rest of your life.

Chapter 3

RECIPE FOR A POLISHED INTRODUCTION

Too many people answer the question "Tell me about yourself!" by taking a literal approach. But the query might actually be better interpreted as "Who are you?" To respond effectively, you need a simple summary of who you are. To sum up your unique talents, your experience and your personal style, you just need a few basic ingredients wrapped in your own personality. We have created three easy-to-remember "factors."

 The Essence Factor: This is the summation of who you are in one sentence.

 The Guru Factor: This lets people know what you know that sets you apart from your peers.

 The Star Factor: This is what you do and how you do it that distinguishes you.

In the next three chapters, we will explore each of these factors in depth. At the end of each chapter is a worksheet to help you to create your Essence, Guru, and Star factors. Once you have each element developed, we help you put it all together to create your Personal Introduction.

PERSONAL INTRODUCTIONS

Just the Facts

To do that, however, you will have to address those cultural, emotional and psychological barriers that make it so hard to craft an effective introduction. A good approach is to shift your perspective so that you focus on the facts—just the facts—rather than your opinion of yourself.

Despite what you may think, describing yourself is *not personal*. It's factual. You need to get comfortable with being able to talk about yourself in a neutral, non-emotional way.

In an interview, for example, you are the "product" you're selling a "customer" who you want to make a "purchasing" decision in your favor. In an important business or personal meeting, you want to establish credibility and likeability in your first few words.

Here are two important concepts that will help.

Be Specific: When speaking of yourself, provide sufficient information so that your audience will conclude you are exceptional. How do you do that? You need to drill down to the specifics. For example, if you are "smart", what does that really mean? Are you someone who sees solutions quicker than others, or are you someone who is really good at defining problems. Are you academically smart or street-smart, or both? Do you have a good memory or aptitude for details?

Use Someone Else's Words—3rd Party Attribution: A remarkably effective and more comfortable way of bragging is by letting someone else do it for you. Instead of describing your outstanding characteristics in the first person (I am . . .), you can draw on statements that others have made or would make about you. For example, rather than stating, "I am an exceptional programmer", John can say "The CIO recently described me as an exceptional programmer." That's a fair statement and far more comfortable to say. And since it was exactly what the CIO said, it's not only factual but more powerful.

Finally, remember that every person brings something special to the table. It's simply a matter of paying attention and allowing yourself to recognize your own talents and accomplishments. No two people are alike, so focus on the unique qualities that you bring to the table.

Chapter 4

YOUR ESSENCE FACTOR

You are at a meeting, seated at a table with a half-dozen other people who are introducing themselves using no more than three or four words such as facilities manager, aerospace engineer, or sales rep. What three or four words would you use to describe yourself?

> **STEP 1: Jot down 3-4 words that you would use to describe your essential qualities as a professional.**

Rather than simply choosing the job you hold today, take a broader perspective. Think about your career, the job you held before this one, and the job that will come next. What words capture your *essential qualities* as a professional? These words are the core of your "Essence Factor".

They should be designed to help people understand you clearly and quickly. Picture this: if you were sorting people into "folders," you might put the engineers into one "folder," the accountants into another "folder," and the airplane pilots

PERSONAL INTRODUCTIONS

into a third. This label will allow people to figure out how to "file you." It's as simple as that.

STEP 2: Add a strong modifier that describes a defining dynamic quality about you.

Find a modifier that you can put in front of those descriptor words. That modifier should convey a strong, dynamic aspect of your abilities. Jot down three or four possible choices that would strengthen your description. Choose the modifier you like best.

Think of this as a powerful stake in the ground that establishes your first impression. Remember, it also needs to stand alone in those few instances when this is all you have time to say.

STEP 3: Create a sentence by adding more specifics about who you are.

Let's assume everyone at the table can introduce themselves with a whole sentence. What would you want to add that gives people a better picture of who you are? It might be something about your industry or an area of your background or a functional specialty. For example, if you are currently a financial professional, you might want to tell people that you have public accounting experience or come from Wall Street. If you are an IT person, you might want to say that you specialize in the oil and gas industry.

Here are some good basic examples of Essence Factors in opening statements.

- Hello. I'm **Sam Chen**, and I'm a certified project manager and operations analyst in the aerospace industry.

- Hi, there. My name is **Nicole Sherrod**. I am a consultant in the Consumer Products practice of Bearing & Light.

- Good morning. My name is **Shana Price**. I'm a national account manager at a pharmaceutical company for a popular line of dermatology products.

BE MEMORABLE

1. Introductions need to be memorable. A good introduction is not boring. Use colorful or powerful adjectives that give you personality.

2. You need to make your name stick. It is *your* responsibility for others to remember who you are, including your name. Is there anything unique about your name? Use it. If you have a more common name, link it to something that is in the news, is connected with the entertainment industry, or will make a connection with your audience. Finally, in a formal networking introduction, remember to repeat your name at the end.

3. What you choose to talk about here must be carefully selected to highlight what matters for *your purpose*. Don't include something that diverts attention from your goals.

4. Slow down and take your time to do a proper introduction. Be articulate, speak to be heard, and make sure that people hear and know how to pronounce your name. Don't rush through this!

PERSONAL INTRODUCTIONS

Your ESSENCE FACTOR Worksheet

Step 1: Jot down 3-4 words that you would use to describe your essential qualities as a professional.

___

Step 2: Add a strong modifier that describes a defining dynamic quality about you.

___

Step 3: Create a sentence by adding more specifics about who you are.

___

Chapter 5

YOUR GURU FACTOR

Most accomplished people have cultivated specific knowledge and functional skills that are uniquely valuable in the marketplace. We call this the "Guru Factor". In a personal introduction, this part provides important distinctions from everyone else—the competition—who might have a similar Essence Factor.

STEP 4: Inventory all your special areas of knowledge.

To figure out your own Guru Factor, think about the things people come to you for when they want your knowledge. For example, if you are a financial person, do they turn to you when they want to know more about SEC reporting or asset valuations? If you are an IT person, you may know more about Cloud-based or mobile applications than others.

Make a list of all your areas of expertise. Consider all possibilities related to your professional focus. What are those areas where you are the "go-to" person in your organization? What do you study? When others research an area, do they call

PERSONAL INTRODUCTIONS

you for information? Do you have technical knowledge or deep understanding in a particular area or subject that enhances your value? These are all candidates to be included in your Guru Factor.

STEP 5: Select your top one or two that are relevant to your goals.

Once you have a comprehensive list, select the top one or two areas of expertise that matters most to your audience. Choose the ones that truly set you apart. These are your Guru Factors.

STEP 6: Create a sentence that clearly communicates your expertise.

Now create a "key word" sentence that provides a context for your expertise. There may be areas of knowledge that you take for granted but nonetheless differentiate you from others. Start with the statement "I have expertise in or in-depth knowledge of . . . ." It might look like this: "I have expertise in SEC reporting as well as in-depth knowledge of foreign currency and commodity hedging."

You met Sam, Nicole and Shana earlier in the book. Here are Guru Factors that they might have constructed:

- *Sam:* I have expertise in logistics and use advanced Excel for supply chain modeling.

- *Nicole:* I'm known as a Six Sigma expert for factory floor processes.

- *Shana:* I have in-depth knowledge of cutting edge aesthetics research.

Some people, however, find it tough to identify their Guru Factor. Don't give up too easily though. While this may be the most difficult to decipher, it can also be an important differentiator.

If you just can't identify one or two areas of expertise, move on to your Star Factor. People who lack a strong Guru Factor will often have several Star Factors.

BE CLEAR

1. Your Guru Factor is about what you KNOW, not what you DO. It addresses your knowledge base, not how you get things done.

2. Not every person will have a Guru Factor. If you don't, leave it out. Increase your emphasis on your Star Factor. Someone who is a "jack of all trades and master of none" may be able to lead teams, mediate problems, or otherwise be very successful in how they do things.

PERSONAL INTRODUCTIONS

Your GURU FACTOR Worksheet

Step 4: List ALL your special areas of knowledge.

Step 5: Select your top one or two that are relevant to your goals.

Step 6: Create a sentence that clearly communicates your expertise.

Chapter 6

YOUR STAR FACTOR

Now that you have laid out the functional and knowledge part of your introduction, you need to share more of your qualitative side. This is your opportunity to motivate someone into a deeper level of engagement. It's your chance to tell them why they would want to hire you, work with you in some other capacity, or recommend you to another colleague.

> **STEP 7: Create a comprehensive list of qualities and attributes that others see in you that set you apart from your peers.**

Think about your Star Factor in the context of how you get things done. It is often about your personal qualities, professional characteristics, and style and how those elements are applied in your work life. Sometimes this is an opportunity to talk about your "soft" skills. As with the Guru Factor, start by making a thorough list of all these characteristics.

Once again, it is important to be specific. What <u>exactly</u> makes you a star? If you find yourself struggling with this, think about what other people have said about

PERSONAL INTRODUCTIONS

you. Consider which ones work well with your other factors, which ones position you best with your audience, and which ones are most closely aligned with your goals. Here are four clusters of questions that might be helpful in thinking about your Star Factor.

- ☐ **Love:** What do you love about what you do? What is your mission, your passion? What about your work gets you up in the morning and keeps you motivated?

- ☐ **Good:** What makes you good at what you do? What innate abilities, unique talents, or special gifts do you have that others don't? How specifically do you think about things that contribute to your success?

- ☐ **Like:** Why do people like to work with you? These people include peers, bosses, employees, internal staff, customers/clients, vendors, regulators, politicians, and others. Why do they buy from you? What do people count on you for?

- ☐ **Say:** What do people say about you (only the good things)? What have your customers said about you? What would a reference say? What positive things have been documented in performance appraisals and letters of recommendation? Why did you receive an award? Why would a former boss rehire or recruit you? How does the press characterize you? In a nutshell, why should I bring you into my organization?

STEP 8: Select just the top few that are clearly outstanding, most important to your success, and consistent with your focus.

Pick the top two or three "personal game changers." You want to distinguish yourself from everyone else who had the same or similar Essence and Guru Factors.

STEP 9: Create one or two sentences that showcase these distinguishing qualities or characteristics.

The "Star Factor" part of your introduction often begins with "recognized for...", "distinguished by...", "known for...", or "others say...". Since the Star Factor is about more personal qualities and attributes, it can be somewhat awkward to talk about. A third party attribution can make this sentence feel less self-aggrandizing or "braggy." They are saying something great about you rather than you saying it about yourself.

Here are some Star Factor examples for Sam, Nicole and Shana:

- *Sam*: People like to work with me because I listen carefully to make sure that I understand deliverables. They also appreciate that I am a real team-player and relationship builder who collaborates with them to get the job done.

- *Nicole:* Clients rely on my advice because of the time I've spent in the field working directly with their employees.

- *Shana:* One of the keys to my success has been my ability to be persistent without being annoying. My customers appreciate that I keep them up-to-date on new products that will be helpful to their patients' demographics.

PERSONAL INTRODUCTIONS

BE SPECIFIC

1. Try to avoid generic words like "leadership skills" or "communication ability". They are too broad and ubiquitous to be distinctive. What <u>exactly</u> do you do that makes you a great leader or outstanding communicator? It is the specifics that set you apart from all the other great leaders and outstanding communicators.

2. The best Star Factors are qualities or characteristics that are atypical for people in your role. For example, if you are an accountant, being detail oriented would be expected, predictable, or even assumed. But an accountant with a great sense of humor and recognized bridge builder would be less common and potentially more compelling.

Your STAR FACTOR Worksheet

Step 7: Create a comprehensive list of qualities and attributes that others see in you that set you apart from your peers.

_____

_____

_____

_____

_____

Step 8: Select just the top few that are outstanding, most important to your success, and consistent with your focus.

_____

_____

_____

_____

Step 9: Create one or two sentences that showcase these distinguishing qualities or characteristics.

_____

_____

_____

_____

Chapter 7

PUTTING IT ALL TOGETHER

Now that you have the ingredients prepared for the Personal Introduction recipe—your Essence, Guru, and Star Factors, it's time to create your masterpiece.

STEP 10: Write it.

Write out a short paragraph using simple, uncomplicated sentences. Use active voice. Make it short and sweet, easy to remember. Make sure it flows smoothly from sentence to sentence.

STEP 11: Talk it.

Once you have *written* your introduction, say it out loud. Make sure that you can comfortably "talk" it. It may be wonderful on paper but very difficult to deliver orally. Longer more sophisticated words with lots of syllables sound awkward and stilted when we say them. Long compound, complex sentences don't come out of our mouths very easily, and we lose our listeners along the way. Use simple sentences. Choose the "real" words that you would actually say rather than the words you write. Feel free to use colloquialisms and color to aid in bringing your words alive.

PERSONAL INTRODUCTIONS

Here are the introductions developed by taking the factors for Sam, Nicole and Shana, putting them together, and refining them for "talkability". Imagine these people are introducing themselves to you.

- Hello. I'm **Sam Chen**, and I'm a certified project manager and operations analyst in the aerospace industry. I have expertise in logistics and use advanced Excel for supply chain modeling. People like to work with me because I listen carefully to make sure that we are all on the same page. They also appreciate that I am a real team player. Relationships are important to me. That's how we get the job done—by working together.

- Hi, there. My name is **Nicole Sherrod**. I am a consultant in the Consumer Products practice of Bearing & Light. I am a Six Sigma expert, especially in manufacturing processes. Clients trust my advice because of the time I've spent in the field working directly with their employees. I have a reputation for working hands-on to really understand what happens on the floor.

- Good morning. My name is **Shana Price.** I'm a national account manager in pharma, and I represent a popular line of dermatology products. I make it a point to stay up to date on current research. People say one of my keys to success is knowing how to be persistent without being annoying. My customers appreciate that I keep them up-to-date on new products that are helpful to their patients.

Notice how these introductions have changed slightly when refined for "talkability". Sentences are a little simpler and easier to say. The best Introductions are crisp, interesting, and short—30 seconds really means 30 seconds—not 3 minutes!

Feel free to add in bits and pieces that show your personality—make it catchy and memorable. What can you do to make yours more interesting? In certain situations, you may want to be more informal or playful. Here are a couple of examples.

- Hi, I'm Harry Stephens. I've been working in advertising and media for most of my career. I love making companies and products irresistible.

- My name is Jennifer Jeffries, and I am a landscape architect at Fortson Services. I've been a champion of wildflower projects on our national highways.

The key here is to craft something that sums you up clearly and professionally. Once that message is clear, make sure you practice, practice, practice. This brief introduction should be so well rehearsed that it doesn't sound rehearsed. A music teacher once said, "Don't practice until you finally get it right. Practice until you can't get it wrong." This helps you display confidence, humor, and positive energy.

Remember, your introduction will always be a work in progress. It will evolve depending on who you are talking to, what your goals are, and how your career develops.

STEP 12: Test it.

Once you have practiced your Personal Introduction alone, try it out on someone else. Remember, effective communication is like a dance. It has rhythm and flow. When you are giving your Personal Introduction, you need to establish rapport with your audience. When you pay attention, you can read the responses of your listeners. Don't talk too fast—a comfortable pace with a few pauses helps your listeners listen.

Ask for honest feedback, and don't settle for easy answers. If you just ask people how they like it, they will often say, "It's fine." This is not helpful. If you give them specific criteria, they can give you helpful feedback.

PERSONAL INTRODUCTIONS

We've created a Personal Introduction Feedback Form that will assist you in getting honest and useful feedback from your listeners.

BE COMPELLING

Your Personal Introduction is the perfect opportunity to motivate someone to help. By having a memorable, clear, and specific introduction, you can give the listener just the right amount of information for them to take action on your behalf. And, it creates that positive first impression that is so crucial.

> BE SHARP!
>
> BE MEMORABLE.
>
> BE CLEAR.
>
> BE SPECIFIC.
>
> BE COMPELLING.

PUTTING IT ALL TOGETHER

Your PERSONAL INTRODUCTION Worksheet

Step 10: Write your first draft by combining all your factors into a seamless paragraph.

Step 11: Say it out loud and change it if needed to make it more "talkable."

Step 12: Try your introduction out with someone and ask for honest feedback. You can use the form on the following page to collect useful, actionable input.

PERSONAL INTRODUCTIONS

Personal Introduction Feedback Form

Would you be willing to listen to my Personal Introduction and give me your honest evaluation? Here are some questions I would like to consider as you listen.

Yes	No	QUESTION	WHAT IT MEANS
		Is it clear?	Do you immediately get a picture of the person being described?
		Is it me?	Do you recognize me, the person you know?
		Is it engaging?	Does it portray me as a person with distinguishing and valuable capabilities and qualities?
		Does it capture the essence of my story?	Does it flow easily into more detail?
		Does it have impact?	Does it have a WOW factor? Does it showcase my talents?
		Was it delivered well?	Did I come across as comfortable and authentic?
		Is it memorable?	Is it catchy and interesting to listen to? Would you remember me?

Reprinted by permission: Yellow Brick Path, Copyright 2017
Readers may copy this form for personal use.

Chapter 8

YOUR INTRO IS A GATEWAY

In various situations, such as job search networking meetings or business development networking events, you may have the opportunity to introduce yourself. This is commonly referred to as your 30-second elevator pitch. The basic difference between this and your core Personal Introduction is the emphasis of your name at the beginning and end and the concluding sentence or two summarizing your "ask" (what you want or something specific they can do to assist you). For example, in a job search, you may be looking for an introduction into a specific department or function at a particular company. In a business networking setting, you may want introductions to prospective customers, such as a recent retiree who may need to roll over a 401(k).

Always start with saying your name clearly—and speak loud enough for everyone to hear you. The more complex your name is, the more important it is to slow down and enunciate. It might even be helpful to provide the listener a way to remember or pronounce your name. For example, "My name is Melissa Cabernay—like the red wine."

Once you have delivered your pitch, repeat your name again at the end along with an easy way for them to contact you if appropriate—maybe your website. This helps people remember you, which after all is the point of the meeting.

PERSONAL INTRODUCTIONS

Until you feel completely comfortable and secure with your pitch, we recommend that you print it out and drop it into your briefcase or portfolio. That way you can review and practice it on the way to important networking events to ensure that it is fresh, polished, and top of mind.

Beyond the Elevator Pitch—the Situational Introduction

A polished Personal Introduction is an essential starting point. However, in certain situations, it is not exactly right. In many settings it is better to build rapport and engage others in conversation based on thoughtfully prepared information and messages than to deliver mini-speeches.

A Situational Introduction is your core personal pitch specifically tailored to who you are talking to, what message or messages you want to deliver, and how much time is available. Rather than viewing an introduction as something to be memorized or read from a teleprompter, you have now developed a basket of material about yourself from which you can pull the relevant pieces to deliver a more refined and targeted introduction. As you get comfortable with talking about yourself, it will be easy for you to "reach in" and get what you need for any particular situation.

For example, if you are at a professional luncheon meeting, you may get only 4 to 6 words and five seconds as attendees around the table introduce themselves. At a networking gathering, you may get 15—20 seconds. At an interview, you may get as much as a minute. Perspectives and agendas will vary depending upon your audience and your goals.

A Situational Introduction provides not only a better application for your personal introduction but also the freedom to relax and let the conversation flow appropriately. You have a multitude of opportunities to practice your pitch and get the word out. Use them. Once you've done the spade work to create a solid Personal Introduction, you're much better equipped to deliver a Situational Introduction that hits the mark.

Pitching Your Business

Pitching your business is almost the same as introducing yourself, but the subject is the business, not you. Even when you are the business (a solopreneur), your messaging should emphasize outcomes and deliverables. In a business networking meeting, you may be invited to stand up and briefly introduce your business. Being well prepared with a concise and memorable description can make all the difference.

Let's apply the basic model for a Personal Introduction to your Business Introduction. Listed below are some of the key questions to ask yourself as you focus on your business.

Your Business' Essence Factor
- What is your business?
- What services and/or products does your business provide?
- What niche does your business serve?

Your Business' Guru Factor
- What specific expertise does your business provide?
- What knowledge base sets you apart from your competitors?

Your Business' Star Factor
- Why do your customers buy from your business?
- How is your business distinguished from others? From your competitors?
- What unique qualities are the hallmarks of the important relationships with your customers, suppliers, employees, or investors?

From Spoken Introduction to Written Positioning

For resumes, bios, and marketing materials, you need a statement or description that establishes an identity aligned with the needs of the organization or the job. This could be in the form of the introductory paragraph of a bio, the summary section of a resume, the opening section of a profile, or the "About" page of a website.

PERSONAL INTRODUCTIONS

This paragraph comes right from your written Personal Introduction, converted to third person ("he/she" versus "I"). Use your full name to start, and then use either your first or last name for subsequent references, depending on how formal you need to be. An increasingly common practice is to use first person ("I") in the summary section of online profiles such as LinkedIn.

Having a clear positioning is the cornerstone of your entire personal "marketing kit." It carries your message consistently throughout all your communications, written and oral. It contributes to your branding—you want it to be strong and memorable.

Pay Attention to the Delivery Medium

Your ability to introduce yourself professionally and smoothly is going to come in handy over and over again. There is an expanding array of avenues in which you will have the opportunity to be visible and capture the attention of an audience. As an evolving practice, these opportunities are no longer limited to networking events, business meetings, and basic job interviews. The world is your stage now. It is imperative that you cultivate a natural and strong presence across diverse environments and platforms.

Some of the media that demand a professional touch and a personal spin are:

- Wide ranging social media profiles, such as LinkedIn, Twitter, and Facebook
- One-way or two-way video job interviews
- Webcasts that are associated with outlets such as YouTube and blogs
- Television interviews where you are a contributing expert
- Creative new avenues we haven't thought of or haven't been invented yet

In order to deliver a polished introduction, pay attention to the unique requirements of the delivery medium and the desired audience experience.

Part Two

PROFESSIONAL BIOS

Chapter 9

WHY DO I NEED A BIO?

Now that you can respond to "Tell me about yourself" in a short paragraph, you may find you that you sometimes need a more detailed answer. That's the role of a professional bio. It puts flesh on the bare bones of your introduction. A professional bio is a valuable personal marketing tool. Its purpose is to help you sell yourself to networking contacts, to prospective employers and to the market in general. A resume is basically a factual chronology, not a narrative. The bio is written in a prose style that allows to you *tell your story*, making it short, sweet, and engaging.

Professional bios have a wide variety of applications. Some of the most common are social media profiles, speakers introductions, business website "about us" pages, sales proposals, marketing brochures, internal announcements and postings, awards and recognitions, press releases, published books and articles, blogs—basically any place where someone needs to know something about you.

With the expanding popularity and applications of social media, the need for a well-written story in the form of a bio is escalating. For example, the first paragraph of your bio can be adapted to create the summary section on your LinkedIn profile. And your key words can be used in your Headline. The use of your personal introduction in social media is covered more thoroughly later in the book.

PROFESSIONAL BIOS

Your bio is like a personal press release. It should entice someone to want to get to know you. Once someone understands your professional story—which is NOT a summary of your life experiences—he or she can go to the resume to fill in the details. The bio gives the reader guidance in understanding how to think about you. The resume provides the details.

Given the plethora of personal information easily available to the global community, it is essential that professionals attend to managing the presentation and content of this information. For those people who have avoided a public presence, it is more important than ever to establish themselves visibly and be in control of the narrative.

Here's a chart that compares the characteristics of a resume with those of a bio.

WHY DO I NEED A BIO?

RESUME	BIO
Typically announces to the world that you're looking for a job.	Applicable to almost any situation. In job search, it's safer to be public without producing unwanted exposure or jeopardy.
It's about details—provides relevant facts about your work history, accomplishments, and credentials.	It's about spin—highlights your most outstanding characteristics and accomplishments and focuses the narrative.
Because it contains more information often not read in detail, it's hard to differentiate what's important and to communicate the story line.	Short, easily readable, absorbed quickly by the reader.
One to three pages, single spaced, relatively small point size.	One page, slightly expanded spacing between lines (1.15—1.5), larger point size, generally 4 paragraphs and 350—400 words.
Primarily a job search tool, both internal and external.	Multi-purpose document that can be used in a wide variety of situations.
Almost everyone should have a resume.	Bios in business are usually associated with senior professionals, executives, and entrepreneurs.
Resume development helps you organize the details of your experiences and refreshes your memory about your capabilities and accomplishments.	Bio development is a uniquely powerful process for learning how to present your professional story in person as well as in writing.

PROFESSIONAL BIOS

When to Use a Bio vs a Resume

There are several good reasons to use a bio before or instead of a resume.

1. Resumes can be seen as public announcements that you are actively job hunting. Bios don't carry the same implication. Thus, a bio could be in anyone's hands for any reason at any time.

2. A resume doesn't tell a professional story—it is an informational document. That means the reader would have to try to piece together your story using the facts in the resume. This would be inefficient and potentially problematic by allowing the readers to come their own conclusions about the real story. By using a bio, you stay in the driver's seat of the message.

3. Too much information can dilute a clear message. Often your goal is to provide just enough information to get people to ask more about you or request your resume.

Resume and Bio—an Example of Each

Take a look at the following sample resume and associated bio to see the differences. The first is a resume for a senior financial executive, and the second is a bio for the same person.

WHY DO I NEED A BIO?

SAMPLE PROFESSIONAL RESUME

JOHN MENDOZA, CPA

Milwaukee, WI—Available to Travel and/or Relocate
4221 Marketplace Road, Shorewood, WI 99999

Fluent in English & Spanish

Phone: 444.555.6666   Email: john.mendoza@email.com
linkedin.com/johnmendoza

SENIOR FINANCIAL EXECUTIVE
Manufacturing and Distribution

Innovative and strategic financial leader. Expertise in strategic investments and operational projects, primarily in the U.S. and Latin American markets. Called on to lead complex corporate programs leveraging his broad experience base and consultative communication style. Counsels teams on better operational and market execution and provides insight to the Board of Directors and executive team on sound business and financial approaches. Integrally involved in determining investor communication strategy and managing the analyst call process.

Global Strategy—M&A—Risk Management—Technology Oversight
"Big Four" Audit Experience

ROI Focused—Metrics Driven—Proactive Decision Maker—Team Builder—Articulate

---

AMERICAN CORPORATION (NYSE:ACO)   2012–Present
$350 million, global manufacturer and distributor of specialty polymer composite materials and components to growing markets. Products are based on core technologies in polymers, fillers and adhesion. www.amcorp.com

Corporate Controller—Corporate Officer, Milwaukee, WI
Manage all public and internal financial and operational reporting, strategic planning and capital administration, financial system implementations and administration, M&A, operation initiatives, and financial service functions. Direct management of 25 corporate finance staff and oversight of over 50 worldwide operational finance professionals.

- Led the successful acquisition and integration of multiple companies ranging from $15 to $85 million in annual revenues. Also led the divestiture of a $35 million nonstrategic business and the start up of an India-based $25 million joint venture
- Led the team that successfully established a $50 million manufacturing and distribution center in Mexico—from Board approval through the start up of operations
- Eliminated over $1.5 million in corporate overhead through streamlining of consolidated reporting systems and processes and improving quality (accuracy, integrity, timeliness) of the executive financial and operational reporting model
- Generated over $5 million in productivity gains by playing a key role in the successful launch of Six Sigma within the organization

PROFESSIONAL BIOS

MAXIMUM INDUSTRIES (NYSE:MSM) www.maximumind.com 2008–2012
$4 billion company that manufactures and sells a wide range of electrical and tools products. www.maxind.com

Division Controller—Tools Division, Los Angeles, CA (2009-2012)
Managed all financial and tax reporting, financial analysis, budget and capital administration, treasury, financial support functions, and internal control administration for the $950 million Tools Division. Direct management of 25 division financial staff and oversight of 200 financial staff within the division operations.
- Drove $1 million in savings from headcount reduction, process streamlining, and system rationalization in leading the reorganization as the company consolidated two divisions
- Completed numerous multi-million dollar strategic initiatives by providing financial project management in acquisitions and integration, operational restructuring, and asset dispositions

Corporate Audit, Senior Manager, Chicago, IL (2008-2009)
Teamed with management in identifying critical business risks and developing innovative business solutions including new ERP system implementations, major joint venture investments in Brazil, new acquisitions, plant expansions/rationalizations, and Corporate reporting
- Reduced audit budget by over $500,000 by redirecting focus to business risk and developed new assurance service tools to deploy the new business risk philosophy
- Instrumental in the $7 million reduction of the purchase price of a major acquisition through due diligence and careful evaluation of market conditions

GMPK INTERNATIONAL 1991–1998
Largest global public accounting firm. www.gmpk.com

Audit Manager, Miami, FL (2006-2008)
Assistant Audit Manager, Mexico City, Mexico (2004-2006)
Supervising Senior Accountant, Miami, FL (2001-2004)
Managed a diverse multinational client base in manufacturing, retail and distribution including a $3 billion publicly traded, global, world-class supplier of power generation equipment and services
- Led the office's first outsourcing of a major client's internal audit function which produced a 25% annual savings for the company and $2 million of incremental revenue for the firm
- Established a firm wide reputation for expertise in the Mexican accounting practices and statutory reporting regulations

EDUCATION & CERTIFICATIONS
MS Accounting, University of Florida, 2004
BBA, Magna cum Laude, University of South Florida, 2000
CPA, State of Florida, 2001

LANGUAGES: Fluent in English and Spanish

WHY DO I NEED A BIO?

SAMPLE MATCHING BIO

John Mendoza, CPA

Corporate Controller & Corporate Officer
American Corporation

Global Manufacturing—Strategy—Risk Management
M&A—Technology Oversight

JOHN MENDOZA is an Innovative and visionary financial leader with expertise in strategic investments and operational projects, primarily in the U.S. and Latin American markets. He is often called on to lead complex corporate programs leveraging his broad experience base and consultative communication style. John counsels teams on better operational and market execution and provides insight to the Board of Directors and executive team on sound business and financial approaches. He is also integrally involved in determining investor communication strategy and managing the analyst call process.

Currently, as Corporate Controller and Corporate Officer for American Corporation, a publicly held global manufacturer and distributor of specialty materials, John manages all financial operations worldwide, including the financial aspects of M&A initiatives. In this role, he led the team that successfully established a $50 million manufacturing campus in Mexico—from Board approval through the start up. He also helped generate over $6.5 million in productivity gains by playing a key role in the successful launch of Six Sigma and by streamlining consolidated reporting systems.

Previously, as Division Controller at Maximum Industries, he drove $1 million in savings from headcount reductions and system rationalizations in leading a reorganization of the finance team. He also served as a Senior Audit Manager where he reduced the audit budget by $500,000 by redirecting focus to business risk and developing more efficient audit tools. He began his career at GMPK International where he rose to the position of Audit Manager. While at GMPK, he spent two years in Mexico City gaining financial reporting expertise in Latin American business environments.

John is a CPA. He holds an MS in Accounting from the University of Florida and a BBA, Magna cum Laude, from the University of South Florida. He is fluent in English and Spanish.

444.555.6666   john.mendoza@email.com

Chapter 10

WHY MOST BIOS ARE BAD

Bios are everywhere—LinkedIn, websites, social media profiles, speaker one-pagers, conference agendas, marketing brochures, sales presentations, and promotional press releases. Yet most of these bios are boring or unfocused, providing little insight into the person behind the bio. These bios say, "Held this job, did this, held that job, did that, went to school there, grew up somewhere, married the high school sweetheart and has 1.8 kids." Even if you are impressed by the credentials of the people in those bios, how engaged are you with the people themselves?

Bios should serve a specific purpose. The content should be designed for a particular audience and to meet a clear objective. The best bios are carefully crafted to focus on the interests of that audience. Unfortunately, most bios are "all purpose" and not appropriately targeted for their intended use.

A reason that bios are not engaging or compelling is that they are sometimes written in a rigid, uninspired format without a full grasp of the impact or desired goal. If data is just dropped into predetermined "fields" or categories, the resulting document will undoubtedly miss the mark. Any bio should be designed with a specific set of objectives in mind. It's useful to ask yourself, "What impact or outcome do I want to achieve for the reader?"

PROFESSIONAL BIOS

Poorly written bios can be too long and too detailed, including a person's entire career and virtually all of his or her accomplishments. The only people who actually like those long detailed bios are headhunters looking for candidates. They see such bios as an easy resource to be used for compiling complete dossiers on key prospects.

Other bios are too short. Sometimes that's precisely what is needed given the constraints of where it will be presented. In those cases, you have to carefully craft the bio with an economy of words that accurately produces the impression you want. Often this is a situation where credentials are important. If you are not limited on the length of your bio, then create it wisely to communicate your personality, strengths, and value proposition.

Chapter 11

THE FOUNDATION BIO

In today's workplace, professionals will almost certainly need a variety of bios—a LinkedIn profile summary, a business bio for marketing materials, a speaker's bio for podium introductions or programs, or a tailored bio for board of directors positions. To create a cohesive theme and message, you should start with a Foundation Bio. This document by itself has extensive applications and also serves as the basis for other versions. Several sample bios are provided at the end of this chapter.

Overview

To the side of your headshot, your bio begins with your formal name in a heading. If you use a nickname, you can switch to that name for the rest of the bio. If you are known ONLY by your nickname, you may elect to use it exclusively throughout the bio instead of your given name. In that case, include your nickname in the heading, such as:

CJ Jones
Charles "CJ" Jones
Charles (CJ) Jones

Next, your heading includes your title and company (if you are employed) or your tag line (if unemployed). Key words are added for either.

The body of the Foundation Bio consists of four paragraphs.

1. Positioning
2. Current or most recent job
3. The rest of your career
4. Credentials

Structuring the paragraphs is straightforward, keeping in mind that the goal of the document is to create "WOW" in the mind of the reader. For example, "WOW, you did that?" "WOW, I'm impressed!" "WOW, I need to talk with you right away." The bio should immediately and accurately create a positive impression of you, portray your distinguishing capabilities and qualities, and communicate your level of responsibility and expertise. Taken as a whole, you want it to showcase an accomplished, polished, and authentic person.

Contact information is provided in the "footer."

You may deviate slightly from this recommended design and structure in order to best present your career and accomplishments.

Heading

The goal of the heading is to describe yourself with laser focus such that your value is grasped immediately by the reader. This information is then supported in the body of the bio.

THE FOUNDATION BIO

The heading will depend on your current job status. If you are *employed*, the heading consists of the following:

> Your Name
> Your Title
> Your Company

If you are *not currently employed*, replace your title and company with a tag line you fashion out of the core of your Essence Factor.

> Your Name
> Your Tag Line

Your tag line is the three to four words that reflect who you are as a professional. Most likely, it is not your prior job title. It focuses on where you are going in the future rather than where you have been in the past. It should provide a clear indication of your level of experience and your functional expertise, if relevant. Sometimes your tag line will include a descriptor or adjective that increases its impact. It is probably not just the functional descriptor of your most recent job. Think bigger, targeted, and future! You want to tell people who you are and where you are going.

Here are some examples of good tag lines for people who are unemployed:

- Global Supply Chain Executive
- National Account Manager—Consumer Products
- Operations-Focused CFO—Manufacturing
- International Project Manager—Defense Industry
- Nationally-Recognized Security Consultant
- Emerging Technology Specialist—Cloud Computing

Key Words

Key words come next. Choose those **four to six** things that together set you apart and define you uniquely. The process of selecting your key words starts with some brainstorming. Don't edit your thoughts until you have a long list.

Ask yourself the following questions:

- What characteristics will be of interest to this particular audience?
- What are your industry's "hot buttons"—those areas where your expertise is most likely to generate a response, perhaps due to a shortage of resources or talent?
- What do you know that few others know?
- Are there some areas of responsibility that define you particularly well?
- In a job search, what capabilities is the hiring manager or market in general looking for?
- What makes you stand out from colleagues who have jobs similar to yours?
- Are there unique attributes that you can offer within this industry?

Choose words or phrases that all have the same level of significance. You should also choose words that are relevant to your next position. So ask yourself which attributes from your brainstorming list define you best? What *search words* might members of your audience use if they were trying to Google the right candidate or person? What characteristics are unique to someone in your role?

Altogether, your heading should give your readers a very clear understanding of who you are even if they don't read further.

Tips for Key Words

Once you have selected your key words, you need to make sure that they are presented in logical order. Cluster related words together. Ultimately, your key words should flow and make good sense.

You will want each key word to be the shortest form of the word that is still plainly recognizable to your readers. Acronyms like CPA, MBA, HTML, and CRM are all common enough that you probably do not need to spell them out and waste valuable space in your key word line.

In other cases, the use of acronyms may depend on your target audience. You can play with the words and abbreviations to get maximum impact in the limited space available. Consider a logistics professional who wants to communicate her expertise in Supply Chain Management. She could use any of the following, depending on her target readers: Supply Chain Management, Supply Chain, or SCM. If most of the readers in her target audience understand SCM, then that's the best choice. But don't take it for granted. And, if you are concerned that some readers might not understand, you always have the option of spelling out acronyms in the body of your bio.

The key words can be arranged in one or two lines. Normally, the main line essentially defines you. If you use a second line, those key words can provide some of the following:

- Specific expertise showing the breadth of your functional capabilities
- Selected in-demand technical expertise
- Breadth of industry experience
- Unique or rare attributes that are important to your readers

Headshot

Your bio is one of the most important places to include a headshot. Your picture allows you to immediately connect to your reader and create a memorable first impression. Despite the belief that photos play into biases and could result in discrimination of some sort, the lack of a photo leaves the reader without any reference point and may play into other negative assumptions. People often wonder why a photo is missing.

PROFESSIONAL BIOS

Pictures engender trust. There is ample evidence that the use of a photo actually improves the interest level by the reader. With the current and anticipated level of transparency across all media, the supposition that you can hide your unique identity is foolish. In fact, consider that if someone instantly rejected you based solely on your picture, would you really want to connect with them?

According to research conducted by LinkedIn (March 14, 2017), "Simply having a profile photo results in up to 21x more profile views and 9x more connection requests."

Whenever someone reads your bio or looks you up on LinkedIn, you are presenting your professional identity to the world. Often this is a person's first impression of you. We recommend that your photo be appropriate for your audience. Normally, for business professionals, we suggest erring on the side of conservativeness. If your target audience is more informal, then a more casual look is acceptable. Just do some research and get in sync with your audience.

We encourage you to consider what will sell well to your audience. For most businessmen, the norm is a photograph in a nice suit and tie with plain background. For most businesswomen, choose a tailored ensemble, groomed hair, light or natural makeup, and jewelry that doesn't distract. If the corporate look isn't applicable, select a business casual look that is appropriate for your profession. Most of all, your eyes, facial expression, and posture communicate a thousand words. Make sure the photograph projects your professionalism and energy.

The photos you post on Facebook, on a dating site, or have professionally taken for your engagement are rarely good choices. Even some professionally taken pictures, including those taken by corporate photographers who come on executive picture day, may not present you at your best. A bad picture is worse than no picture at all. Take the time and spend the money if necessary to get it right.

A professional headshot should be cropped at your upper arms with the focus on your face. It is a head shot after all, not a book cover photo. Here are some additional guidelines to consider.

Headshots can be taken by a professional photographer or by a friend or family member with experience using a camera. Carefully choose the right backdrop. People will make instant judgments about you when they view your headshot. The person looking at the photo should feel engaged with you. You should expect that people will go look at your LinkedIn profile specifically to see your picture and to get more information about you. As we know, "you never get a second chance to make a first impression."

PROFESSIONAL BIOS

SAMPLE HEADINGS AND KEY WORDS—INDIVIDUALS CURRENTLY EMPLOYED

Roy Walker
Senior Consultant
Herron and Boles Consulting
Large-Scale Cost Reduction Projects—Post-Merger Integration

Alan Chen
Member of Technical Staff
Massachusetts Research Corporation
Program Management
Infrastructure Solutions—Modular Pre-Fab

Keisha Taylor, CPA
Controller
McHenry Corporation
Accounting Operations—Financial Systems Conversions
Food Service—Inventory Control—Scorecard

Sally Smith
District Manager, Southeast Region
ARZ Furniture Mart
Sales & Account Management
District ranked #1 last 3 years

Note on Headshot Placement

Your picture should be integrated into the document alongside your name, heading and key words. Place your headshot on the right or the left so that your head and shoulders are facing into the document rather than off toward the outside margin. The first set of samples shows one position for the headshot and the second is the opposite placement. If both your head and shoulders are facing straight ahead, then you can use whichever placement, right or left, you prefer.

THE FOUNDATION BIO

SAMPLE HEADINGS AND KEY WORDS—INDIVIDUALS IN TRANSITION

Luis Menendez, PMP
IT Development and Quality Assurance Project Leadership
Systems Development Life Cycle (SDLC)
IT Roadmap—ERP—Agile

Kayla Jones
Non-profit Housing Executive
Community Development
Section 8 Multi-family—Lead Hazard
Remediation—Weatherization

James Jackson
Airport Operations & Maintenance Management
FAR 139 Certified Airport—Military Airfield
FAA Rules—Safety Inspections—Project Management

Zia Nanda
Strategic Sourcing Management
Procurement—Supply Chain
Direct & Indirect Spend—Goods & Services—Capital Projects

PROFESSIONAL BIOS

Paragraph 1: Positioning

Having a strong, high-impact positioning paragraph creates an engaging connection with the reader and lays out the most important messages you want to communicate. This is where your story comes to life. It might be tempting to rehash selected competencies or experiences, so you need to stay focused on your message and target audience.

The first paragraph is essentially your Personal Introduction (developed in Part I) converted to third person. You start with your full name and then use either your first or last name for subsequent references, depending on how formal you need to be.

Obviously the first sentence of the first paragraph is the most important. You have already developed it as your Essence Factor. Here are some additional examples for how the Essence Factor is used in the first sentence.

- Roberta Robinson is a retail regional manager with keen understanding of financials, markets, and people.

- Andrew Anton is a business-savvy human resources manager with extensive background in compensation, benefits, and training.

- Gabrielle Vincent is a non-profit housing manager specializing in community development with a conviction that safe homes are fundamental to life success.

- Henry Smith is a hands-on brand manager who grasps a 50,000-foot vision and executes at 50 feet.

- Javier Garcia is an advertising account manager who is attuned to how words and images communicate stories, experiences, and feelings.

- Raj Jindal is a business analyst with experience in data center operations. He has a natural ability to discover the real story from the numbers and understand implications of trends over time.

If you are an executive, make sure this description properly reflects your position and authority in the organization. If it doesn't, you will want to "power up" your description to reflect you actual level of experience and the full range of your accomplishments. Here are some examples of *powerful* first lines.

- Sophie Martin is a pioneer in healthcare informatics.

- Jayla Wilson is a consulting partner who has spent her career driving large global projects.

- Dr. David Smythe is an internationally respected scientist, entrepreneur, educator, and research mentor.

The balance of your first paragraph is the additional information you developed from your introduction: Guru Factors and Star Factors. Make sure this paragraph captures the imagination and interest of the reader. As a reminder, here are some questions from Chapter 6 to consider in order to coalesce the best information.

- What do you love about what you do?
    - What is your mission, your passion?
    - What about your work gets you up in the morning and keeps you motivated?

- What makes you good at what you do?
    - What innate abilities, unique talents, or special gifts do you have that others don't have?
    - How specifically do you think about things that contribute to your success?

- Why do people like to work with you? Not just subordinates but also peers, bosses, customers/ clients, vendors, regulators, politicians, etc.

- What do people say about you?
    - What would a reference say?
    - What positive things get documented in performance appraisals and letters of recommendation?

Take a look at the sample bios to get a better understanding of this important first paragraph.

Paragraph 2: Current or Most Recent Job

Starting with "Currently as..." or "Most recently as..." [your title], indicate the nature of the company's business and a summary of your responsibilities. Here's an example:

"Currently serving as Controller for SimFab, a publicly held manufacturer and distributor of specialty materials, Stefan manages all financial operations including financial analysis and post-acquisition integrations."

The next sentence needs to summarize the most stunning accomplishment you've had in that job. What did you achieve that changed the company, changed the world, or rocketed you into stardom? Think of this sentence as the equivalent of a press release. You get to cherry pick the achievements you wish to highlight. A second sentence may be used to emphasize one additional significant accomplishment. Remember, in the entire bio you will be able to talk about only three to four accomplishments, so make each one of them count.

Depending on your career history, this paragraph can be about your most recent job, all jobs at the same company, or the most important job you had at this company. The goal is to balance this paragraph with the next paragraph and effectively highlight your experience in the right context.

Be Careful

Numbers: Any sensitive corporate information, especially financial numbers, strategic programs, or company statistics that are not a matter of public record and that could provide confidential or competitive information, should NOT be included in your bio. Your bio is not the place for Wall Street analysts to discover what your company is doing or planning to do. In some instances, you can use wording like "multi-million dollar," percentages, or other general descriptors to describe your achievement.

Customers: It may, for example, be advantageous to name names. If you are or were in a job like a Strategic Account Executive responsible for important customers, you will be credentialed by the customers that you handled. If that is a matter of public record, you should consider using their names as part of your description. For example, "Jose was the Major Account Executive for the technology industry. His accounts included Google and Microsoft." It would not be appropriate, however, to disclose the exact dollar amount of each account, nor is it really necessary. The scale and reputation of such companies speak for themselves. In some cases with confidentiality limits, it may not even be appropriate to mention the company names. In this situation, you can describe the company in broad terms. For example, "Sarah is Program Manager for next generation solutions. She is currently working on a team with a global auto manufacturer to integrate artificial intelligence into their automobiles."

Jobs: If your most recent job was off track, not successful, or inconsistent with your future plans, you will want to say as little about it as possible. After mentioning that job, immediately focus on the next most recent job. Hopefully that will have been more interesting and more successful. If you have had a series of bad jobs in the last few years, then you can merge them into a "topic". For example, "Over the last few years, Tony has held marketing positions at Company A, Company B, and Company C." Or "Over the last few years, Sophie has held consulting positions with well-respected boutique firms serving the high tech sector." Regardless of recent problems in your work history, you must have had some "wow" events or accomplishments somewhere in your career. Talk about them.

PROFESSIONAL BIOS

Paragraph 3: Prior Experience

This is the place to sum up the rest of your career, all in *one* paragraph. We know that's a tall order—it can be done, and that's what you have to do. It's not as hard as you think. The goal is to design a paragraph that flows from and works with the previous paragraph. First, review the rest of your career and identify those "high impact" accomplishments that are aligned with the job you desire. Then, decide what message you want to deliver about your skills and contributions, consistent with your target job. Remember, this is an advertisement for you.

This paragraph often begins with either "Previously, . . ." or "Prior to . . ." Here's an example:

> "Previously, Kim was Director of Marketing at Company Q where he led strategic marketing initiatives for global expansion. In this role, he positioned the company for its entry into the Chinese widget market."

Again, this is a place to tell how you saved the world, saved the company, or were responsible for a major breakthrough. If you were an individual contributor and your accomplishments were measured more by the projects you were associated with than your personal work, then you can credential yourself through the whole project. For example:

> "Previously, Gretchen was an engineer with Company R. She participated on the team that developed the one of the first cost effective commercial wind-turbines."

Here's another way: "She was a critical contributor to the project that. . . ."

Some people may have another sequence like this:

> "Earlier Margaret was a project manager with MetroBank and led an international systems development team when the bank expanded its credit card business overseas."

The last sentence of this paragraph will be a simple statement about the beginning of your career to complete the chronology. Yes, it is important to go all the way back to the beginning. But it is one simple sentence, not a paragraph. For example: "Ari began his career as a systems programmer with Company Z."

Paragraph 4: Credentials

For most people, education will be an essential part of this paragraph usually placed at the beginning or end depending on how important it is relative to other credentials. Usually you will lead with your most important, impressive and relevant credentials.

For your education, you may start the sentence this way: "Sam holds a BS in Biology from XYZ University." If you have multiple degrees, it becomes a list: "Carly holds an MS in Taxation from PQR University and a BS in Accounting from ABC University." It is customary and permissible to use shorthand designations—BS, BA, MS, MBA. However, if your degree is somewhat uncommon or not readily known to your audience, you may want to spell it out completely. Not everyone knows that a BFA is a Bachelor of Fine Arts. Surprisingly, there are several different "MM" degrees: Master of Mathematics, Master of Music, Master of Ministry, Master of Management, and more.

Degrees from other countries are often named differently and should be spelled out *along with* the domestic equivalent for comparison purposes.

If you don't have a degree but are college educated, you may say that you "received your education at GGG University." If you have not attended college or took only a few hours of classes, then just leave it out. Emphasize your other credentials.

This paragraph also includes any other credentials that you may have that are relevant and meaningful.

For example, do you have any of the following?

- Certifications: CPA, PMP, CFA, CISSP
- Awards—Internal: President's Club, Leadership Award, Top Salesperson
- Awards—External: Small Business of the Year, Most Valuable Volunteer
- Languages: Spanish, Chinese, Italian (Fluent? Conversational? Has working knowledge of?)
- Publications: Articles, Books, Blogs
- Speaking Engagements: Workshops, Keynote Addresses, Panelist
- Leadership or Memberships: Civic, Industry, or Charitable Organizations (Do you have 'wow' accomplishments with any of these?)

Think Carefully

Faith-based Affiliations

If your community involvement is in faith-based organizations, you need to be careful how you present the information, if at all. This decision is purely personal and will depend on both the circumstances and your audience. It may be completely appropriate in some situations and inappropriate in others. Readers have biases, so tread carefully and judiciously. Use what is most relevant and aligned with your objective.

Interests and Hobbies

If you have interests in which you have a level of leadership or achievement that reflects appropriately on your professional stature, then you should include them. For example, "Harry was the Captain of the U.S. Olympic Equestrian Team." That shows both leadership and an impressive level of dedication and achievement. Riding the trails on weekends doesn't.

Things to Leave Out

In a professional bio, it is not appropriate to include your age, marital status, family, religion, political affiliation, sexual preference, or family's place in the social register. In general these characteristics are not appropriate in a professional setting but could be included if they are specifically relevant to your audience and purpose.

Test Your Bio

Just like you did with your Personal Introduction, once you have written your bio, you should ask people for feedback. As explained earlier in the book, if you request unstructured feedback (How do you like this? What do you think?), you will get "Looks good to me" or "It's fine." That is not helpful.

If you give people specific guidelines for their evaluation, you will get information that will help you refine your bio and make sure that it is on target. You can use the same questions and feedback form that you used earlier.

Remember, the more you test your bio, the better the end result.

The Final Test

- If you received this bio, would you be interested in meeting this person?
- Would you be willing to forward it to a colleague for an open position, a speaking engagement, or other consideration?
- Is this person someone you would hire to provide the services you need for your company, your department, or your project?
- Are you excited about you?

PROFESSIONAL BIOS

Sample Bios

Included on the following pages are several sample foundation bios. We've tried to offer a broad selection so that you may see how the principles outlined in this book have been applied for different people. Of course, as you create your bio, you have to add contact information, usually in a footer at the bottom of the page. Include at a minimum your phone number and email address. Also, if you are using the bio in conjunction with your resume, keep the font and overall design consistent.

Author Paula Asinof obtained permission from several clients to include their bios in *Be Sharp* with their contact information removed. They are presented as they were written at the time of creation, and accordingly their situation is likely different now different as you are reading this book. One client permitted his bio to be included after we adapted and anonymized some of the content. These bios span a variety of industries, functions and positions. Each one follows the same *Be Sharp* recommended structure for the body text. Specifically they show four (and in one instance five) paragraphs covering Positioning, Current or Most Recent Position, Rest of Career, and Credentials.

The heading has been customized using descriptors, key words and tag lines to best present each client. Most headshots have been placed to the right or the left so that they are facing into the document. In two sample bios, the client chose not to use this approach. As reflected in the diverse selection of samples, the basic format provides structure while allowing opportunities for creativity in developing the best and most impactful overall design and content.

- Mark Bailey, Distinguished Engineer—Modular Infrastructure Solutions, Dell EMC

- Kwan Bolton, Gameplay Designer, Magic Games

THE FOUNDATION BIO

- Karen Fricker, Director of Organizational Development & HR North America, Independent Purchasing Cooperative, Inc. (IPC)

- Daniel Hammons, CPA / Independent Consultant, Forensic Accounting & Ownership Structuring

- Mary Martin, Director, Minister of Missions, Grace Avenue United Methodist Church

- Gerald Mathews, Director of Research & Business Development, Forefront Magazine

- Joan Axelrod Siegelwax, EVP Sales, National Accounts & Specialty Channels, Bello LLC

- Patrick Wright, Farm Manager/Ambassador, Bonton Farms

MARK M. BAILEY

Distinguished Engineer, Modular Infrastructure Solutions
Dell EMC

Data Center Architecture Solution Design
Named on 26 Patents

Modular Pre-Fab—Cloud, Edge and Fog Computing Infrastructure
Information Technology—Power Management—Thermal Management

MARK BAILEY is a talented and deeply experienced engineer who blends technical rigor with the cultivation of deep customer and partner relationships. From a holistic and vertically integrated perspective that leads to innovative designs, he drives value-based solutions derived from direct customer feedback and requirements. He is an articulate and engaging communicator who breeds confidence in teams, customers and company leadership though technical competence and consistent delivery. Mark brings out the best in others through careful listening, intellectual stimulation, and culture building.

Currently as Distinguished Engineer, Modular Infrastructure Solutions at Dell EMC, Mark composes the companywide modular infrastructure technology roadmap, strategy, supply chain and fulfilment models for both domestic and global solutions. He not only works with strategic customers to extract design requirements and architect bid responses but also owns the company technology and strategies for cloud, edge and fog-positioned modular infrastructure solutions. In this role, he has diversified the technology portfolio and supplier capabilities as well as forged partnerships with leading innovative companies to optimize integrated solutions for customers worldwide.

Previously as a member of Dell's technical staff, he served as owner of technical content for all modular infrastructure solutions including mechanical, electrical, regulatory, and life-safety elements. He was instrumental in growing business revenue by driving technology improvements, expanding the customer base, and maintaining cost-effective design rigor.

Earlier, as a Dell senior principal engineer, Mark pioneered new engineering mechanics to deploy datacenter infrastructure in 25% of the time and as low as 50% of the cost as compared to traditional builds. He was a member of the team that led to Dell's achieving the first UL-Listing for a modular datacenter, based in part on design rigor. Mark's earlier career spanned mechanical and thermal engineering roles in Dell's Server Solution line of business.

Mark received a BA in Mechanical Engineering from the University of Wisconsin—Madison and an MBA from the University of Phoenix. He is named on 26 patents in Information Technology and Modular Data Centers.

KWAN BOLTON

Gameplay Designer
Magic Games

Video Game Design
Core Experience Design | Prototyping | R&D
Product Pitch Development

Multiple Shipped Product Credits
AAA Quality Titles

KWAN BOLTON is an innovator and creative problem solver who thrives in a vibrant environment working with groundbreaking technology to pave the way for future flagship products. He brings experienced-based knowledge of gaming technologies as well as development methodologies such as rapid prototyping, live ops production, and Agile/Scrum. Kwan balances a collaborative and empowering style with hands-on product involvement. He is respected for fostering a positive team culture even under tight deadlines and changing requirements.

Kwan is a Gameplay Designer with Magic Games located in the UK where he is the Product Owner of an unannounced vehicle-driving AAA title. Currently he is involved in early prototyping in software to prove key concepts. Among the areas where he also has contributed in this role are the feel of second-to-second gameplay, tuning cameras, and surface physics.

Previously Kwan progressed through QA testing and design roles at NextGen Games. As an Assistant Designer, he was mentored by the company's creative director as he worked on early concept including level design sketching and later on greenlight pitch presentations. During his time in QA, he rose from QA Senior Tester to QA Test Lead to Senior QA Test Lead focused on flagging risk areas, enhancing the QA process and writing a QA guide that was ultimately used throughout the company. Earlier he held roles as a Studio QA Embedded Tester for Bright Arts and as a QA Technician with SODIE. He began his career with a short stint as a web designer.

Kwan received a BS in Entertainment Technology from the Illinois Institute of Art, where he graduated 2nd in his class. He has extensive software expertise with shipped titles on all platforms: PS4, PS3, Xbox One, Xbox360, PC, Wii, 3DS and iOS. He is experienced at developing on EA's Frostbite engine and Schematics scripting tool and has a working knowledge of Maya and road building level design tools. Kwan is also proficient in Macromedia Products, Adobe Creative Suite and Microsoft Office.

PROFESSIONAL BIOS

KAREN FRICKER
SPHR/SHRM-SCP

Director, Organizational Development & HR, North America
Independent Purchasing Cooperative, Inc. (IPC)

HR Executive—Foodservice Industry

High Growth—Hourly Through Executive—Non-Union/Union
Talent Management—Employee Development—Recruitment—Retention

KAREN FRICKER blends knowledge of human resources with data that comes from the implementation and use of good tools and insight gained from listening. She is a quick learner with an intuitive sense for connecting the dots. With a gift for enhancing culture and performance, Karen rapidly assesses issues, identifies solutions that get to the core of problems, and acquires the right talent. She cares deeply about people and is committed to doing the right thing for the employees and for the company. Karen strives for the moments when others "get it"—through presentations, training or personal interaction.

Currently, Karen is the Director of Organizational Development and Human Resources for North America, for Independent Purchasing Cooperative (IPC), an independent, member-owned cooperative providing purchasing and IT services for SUBWAY® franchisees. Since joining the company, she has built a human resource function from the ground up with a mission-critical focus on talent acquisition, development, and retention. In support of the company's recent dramatic growth, she promoted 28 staff members and hired 52 new employees in 9 months in an increasingly competitive labor market while maintaining a 92% retention rate. She also achieved a 5-year period of "zero cost" increases in overall benefit expenses and led the organization's space planning and construction process for increasing work space from 25,000 to 60,000 sq. ft.

Previously, Karen was the Senior Director of Human Resources for Sodexo's Healthcare Food & Facilities Division covering 1,200 exempt and 8,200 non-exempt union and non-union employees across twenty states. She provided human resources leadership for the company's mission-critical talent acquisition and evolving culture of diversity and inclusion. Karen began her career at Aramark in food service management and human resources.

Karen received a BS from Eastern Illinois University and holds an SPHR/SHRM-SCP. She is a member of the Society for Human Resources (SHRM), Association for Talent Development (ATD), and Women in Foodservice. Her speaking engagements include serving as a panelist for the Greater Miami Chamber of Commerce on "The Sharing Economy—HR Insights".

THE FOUNDATION BIO

DANIEL R. HAMMONS, CPA

Currently Licensed to Practice in Arizona
Transitioning License to Oklahoma

CONSULTING ENGAGEMENT MANAGEMENT
INTERIM FINANCIAL MANAGEMENT
Forensic Accounting
Financial Organization Evaluation & Restructuring
Corporate & Top Tier Public Accounting Experience

DANIEL HAMMONS is a financial leader with a strong record of achievement in the dynamic and challenging world of forensic accounting and organizational structuring. He is recognized as instrumental in the success of organizations—both the financial function and the company as a whole. With a gift for building rapport and trust, he thrives on working with people and is skilled in conflict resolution. Daniel has outstanding analytic skills, a "think before speaking" approach to business communications, and always delivers on commitments.

Currently, Daniel is consulting with small to medium companies needing expertise and guidance in finance matters such as forensic accounting, ownership structuring, implementation of accounting and reporting systems, and financial personnel evaluation. Key engagements include retention as a forensic accounting expert by the plaintiff in a defamation lawsuit against an investment loss. This project included reconstructing 16 years of accounting records, reviewing Big 4 accounting firm audits, and issuing a Calculation Report. He also consulted on the ownership transition for a multi-site automobile dealership where he provided pre/post-acquisition financial analysis, due diligence, and review of accounting and reporting systems. He was instrumental in the rapid turnaround of the company from a significant loss to break-even. Also, he negotiated interim financing on behalf of the client. Previously he was the CFO of Wilburton State Bank, a community bank serving rural Oklahoma.

Earlier, Daniel was the VP & CFO and company officer with equity participation at Desert Troon Companies, a global real estate developer of commercial office, retail, and lifestyle properties. He oversaw accounting and financial operations, domestic and international tax filings, investor relations, lender relationships, and human resources. He was instrumental in an overall increase of assets from $30 million to $800 million. Daniel also established an investment relationship with one of Arizona's largest pension funds and grew an initial investment of a $12 million 10% participation loan to a direct equity investment of $500 million.

Daniel received a BS with distinction in Accounting from East Central Oklahoma University. He is a CPA currently licensed to practice in Arizona and transitioning his license to Oklahoma. He is affiliated with the American Institute of Certified Public Accountants (AICPA) and with the Societies of Certified Public Accountants in Oklahoma and Arizona.

PROFESSIONAL BIOS

MARY MARTIN

Director, Minister of Missions
Grace Avenue United Methodist Church

COMMUNITY OUTREACH—MISSION DRIVEN ORGANIZATION
Outcome-Driven Program & Case Management
Interdisciplinary Team Environment

SIGNIFICANT NONPROFIT VOLUNTEER EXPERIENCE
International Child Care Board of Directors, Grace Children's Hospital, Haiti
Collin County Homeless Coalition Member, Interfaith Task Force

MARY MARTIN is a mission-driven professional who blends dedication to serving people with well-developed administrative and management skills. She drives positive outcomes and gets the job done by helping people move from "point to point" and achieve measurable improvement. Guided by organizational goals, she leads teams and projects through to completion by priority setting, structured planning, attention to detail and mindfulness of deadlines. Mary is a relationship builder with an authentic, compassionate and personable style.

Over the past decade, Mary has been a rising star in the United Methodist Church as reflected in her selection as pastor-in-charge of two churches in North Texas. Currently, she serves as the Director of Missions at the Grace Avenue United Methodist Church, a 2,600-member congregation. In this role she leads the creation and implementation of programs and ministries that address local and global concerns, serving the poor and underserved populations. She began her ministry career as Director of Adult Ministries at the First United Methodist Church of Allen.

Earlier, Mary utilized her license as an Occupational Therapist in both patient care and administration. As an administrator, she was the Director of Operations and Clinic Manager of the "Return to Work" Program at the Texas Back Institute and Director of Therapeutic Services at the North Texas Medical Center, now part of Medical City of McKinney. Focus in these roles included case management, streamlining workflows, optimizing patient management, and achieving patient care outcome goals.

Mary holds a Master of Divinity from the Perkins School of Theology at Southern Methodist University as well as a Bachelor of Science in Occupational Therapy from Texas Woman's University. Recently she completed a course in grant writing from CNM Connect, a nonprofit management consulting and training firm. Mary also received Disney Institute Certifications in Leadership Excellence and Quality Services.

THE FOUNDATION BIO

GERALD MATHEWS

Director of Research & Business Development
Fore*front* Magazine

"Profiles are the stories that inspire"

GERALD MATHEWS loves a good story. Using the "profile" as a vehicle for telling them, he brings one-of-a-kind successes to life for his readers. With a flair for the creative, Gerald is constantly finding new ways to communicate ideas and engage his audience. His talent for listening, understanding, creating a story, and conveying it to others is a key foundation of his success. Publishing is the perfect venue for turning his talents into successful business ventures.

Currently, Gerald is Director of Research and Business Development at Fore*front* Magazine, an online leadership publication that showcases exciting and talented leaders in profile-driven articles. In this role, he identifies and engages senior executives for profiles in the magazine. Gerald unearths those with unique stories and exceptional accomplishments that provide readers with motivation and insight for furthering their careers.

Previously, Gerald was Director of Sales and Research for Bowen Enterprises, a spin-off of Guerrero Howe Custom Media where he served in Sales and Account Management. At Bowen, he led the re-launch of the print editions of Luxury Home Quarterly Magazine and its sister publication Luxury Home Canada. He created innovative ways to feature homes along with their builders, architects, and designers, including adding regional focus and themes to each issue. He was instrumental in increasing exposure for the publication and growing advertising revenues.

Gerald holds a BA from the University of Michigan, Ann Arbor where he majored in English Literature. He also completed a program of Pre-Med coursework and began his career working in physical therapy.

PROFESSIONAL BIOS

JOAN AXELROD SIEGELWAX

EVP Sales, National Accounts & Specialty Channels
Bello, LLC

Foodservice Industry
BUSINESS DEVELOPMENT—ACCOUNT GROWTH—TURNAROUNDS

CHANNEL MANAGEMENT
Distribution & Brokers
C-Store—Business & Industry—Chains—Military—Airlines

JOAN AXELROD SIEGELWAX is the consummate sales executive with a long history of personal sales success, an impressive record of developing talent and deep industry connections that drive innovative solutions and customer successes. She thrives on her time at customer sites working collaboratively to find the right products for their businesses. A good listener who genuinely cares about people, Joan steps up with confidence to difficult conversations. She excels at bringing clarity to complex issues, turning around underperforming areas, and building high performing organizations.

Currently, Joan is EVP Sales for National Accounts & Specialty Channels for Bello LLC that recently acquired Love and Quiches, a 43-year-old international food manufacturing company that creates custom quiches and desserts for all facets of the food service industry. She leads sales initiatives and provides leadership to the next generation that drive acquisition and growth of key accounts— including specialty channels—for customers such as the U.S. Military, Friday's, Amtrak and Royal Caribbean Cruise Line. Joan consistently drives sales increases of up to 50% in major accounts. For the military, each year she has taken the most on-trend flavor profiles and re-engineered the products to military standards so that combat personnel can enjoy a taste of home.

Previously, Joan progressed through a series of roles in the company gaining expertise in sales, marketing, and product management. She was a leader in delivering sales across numerous high profile accounts through personal performance, team leadership and industry visibility. She was known for gaining a deep understanding of her customers' businesses and taking a consultative approach to selling. Working closely with purchasing, R&D and marketing, Joan delivered innovative solutions that contributed to growing customers' top and bottom lines.

Joan received a B.A. in Marketing and Public Relations from Boston University along with certifications in Digital Marketing and Leadership Development from New York University. She is a member of the Women's Foodservice Forum and has served on the organization's Sponsorship and Membership Committees. She has also organized and led foodservice sales conferences. In conjunction with the local food bank, Joan has been instrumental in establishing "Cake for Kids" that provides birthday cakes to children who would otherwise not have them.

THE FOUNDATION BIO

PATRICK WRIGHT

Farm Manager/Ambassador
Bonton Farms

Diligent and committed to transforming his life and the lives of others
Loves to be part of people breaking through barriers and winning

Bonton Farms and Patrick's Story
https://www.youtube.com/watch?v=IYcOyQ73wUE

"Come stand firm with Patrick"

PATRICK WRIGHT found a home at Bonton Farms that enabled him to rise from the darkness of his life, start all over again, find the goodness inside himself and bring it to realization. Two and half years ago, he stepped onto the farm and the transformation began. Starting as a volunteer and with the unconditional support and spiritual fellowship of the farm community, he put in the hard work and dedication that has molded him into the person he is today and into his role as the Farm Manager and Ambassador.

As the Farm Manager, Patrick is responsible for all the daily operational functions including making sure the animals are taken care of—from food and water to health to supplies purchasing. On the garden side, he makes sure the plants and the 60 fruit trees are healthy, pruned, de-weeded, fed and watered and reaching their potential through proper nutrition. He also maintains the compost bins. In addition, he participates in business activities to bring in restaurants, the community and walk-ins that provide the revenue to continue building the farm.

As Ambassador, Patrick gives regular tours of the farm to groups of children and adults from schools, churches, colleges and businesses. His charismatic personality and his love for the farm engages people from all walks of life to volunteer, donate and "spread the word". Patrick creates loyal followers, and he facilitates real relationships across cultural and racial lines. This has contributed to the incredible transformation of Bonton into a better community for its residents and ultimately affects the vitality of the City of Dallas. The people who come to the farm are from various countries, ethnic and racial backgrounds, ages and interests—and they all become friends there.

Patrick's true love is working with the children. Whether he is showing them the farm, teaching them about organic gardening or letting them feed the goats, he thrives on seeing the kids' excitement as they get engaged. His spirit and the response he gets is well documented in pictures and comments on the Bonton Farms website (www.bontonfarms.org) or its Facebook page.

Part Three

BEYOND THE BASIC BIO

Chapter 12

VARIETY OF BIOS AND APPLICATIONS

Bios, bios, and more bios. . . there are a wide variety of applications for your bio. They range from very short 50-word bios for seminar brochures to comprehensive credential-heavy bios for Board of Director opportunities. While they are different in meaningful ways, they can all be readily developed from your Foundation Bio.

BEYOND THE BASIC BIO

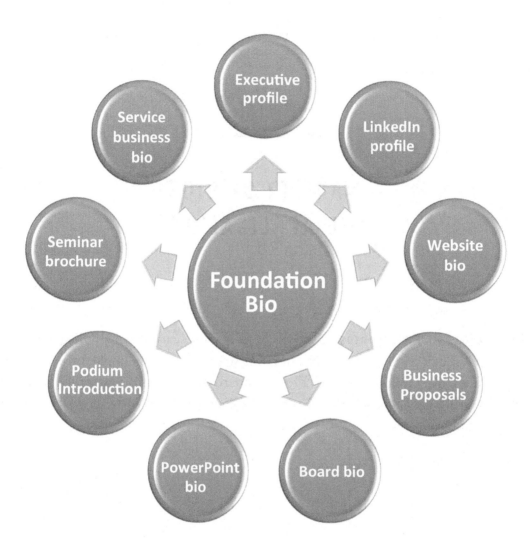

For a better understanding of what the actual documents look like, here is a selection of sample page layouts that show the key differences between the foundation bio and other applications. If the bio is going to be used as part of a group of bios, such as a panel presentation, the length and content of the bio should follow the guidance of the organizer, be consistent with one another, or follow applicable precedent.

VARIETY OF BIOS AND APPLICATIONS

Foundation Bio

- Heading
- Positioning
- Current Job
- Rest of Jobs
- Credentials

- One page
- Picture on one side balanced by heading and key words on the other
- Four approximately equal paragraphs written in third person
- 350-400 words in the body
- Footer with contact information

Board Bio

- Heading
- Positioning
- Current Job
- Rest of Jobs
- Credentials
  Credentials that qualify you for board membership are key

- The same as the Foundation Bio, except the allocation of space between paragraphs three and four.
- The "Rest of Jobs" is less important, and "Credentials" are much more important.

BEYOND THE BASIC BIO

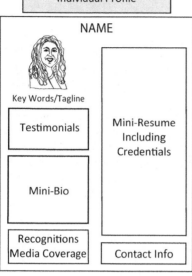

- One page, two columns
- Testimonials are optional
- Mini-Bio of 100 – 150 words
- Mini-Resume is condensed version of regular resume emphasizing key companies, positions and accomplishments, arranged chronologically with years

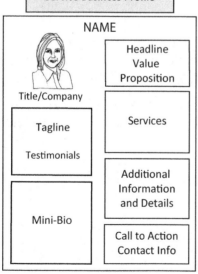

- One page, two columns
- Left column is about the owner
   - One – three testimonials add credibility
   - Mini-Bio of 100 – 150 words
- Right column is about the business

Chapter 13

BIOS FOR JOB SEARCH

There are certain situations where a bio is a better document to use than a resume. The two primary applications are:

1. **Networking:** Your bio allows you to share your story with your networking contacts in a way that optimally presents you and your focus. Also consider whether the other person needs or wants your resume at this stage of your job search.

2. **Job jeopardy:** If you are currently employed and conducting an "unannounced" job search, using a bio rather than a resume is a more discreet way to provide colleagues and potential employers your information. You can share your bio with anyone at any time for any reason, whereas your resume sends the message "I'm looking for a job."

Bios are typically distributed in one of two ways.

- Handed to someone in person
- Sent as an email attachment

BEYOND THE BASIC BIO

While electronic communication and digital formats are increasingly mandated, there still are important occasions or situations when you need to have a hard copy document or a separate file that can produce a printed document.

Handed to Someone in Person

Statistics show the majority of jobs, almost at any level, are obtained through networking. For networking with colleagues, friends, or friends of friends, a bio can be an invaluable tool. Although you will primarily use your business cards at networking events, you will want to take your printed bio and resume to any one-on-one meetings. Of course, the printed document should be professional, nicely formatted, and on quality paper.

In these private meetings, you want to share your background and objectives quickly so that you can focus on deeper levels of conversation. The benefits of sharing your bio at the start of these meetings or in advance are:

1. It will prevent you from spending your entire meeting talking about your history.

2. Properly written, it should engage your contact, making clear the contributions you can make.

3. It's one page, short, and has the critical information they need. That means people can keep it and pass it along to others, if appropriate.

4. If you are currently employed, the bio is a safer way to provide potential employers with initial information.

Sent as an Email Attachment

As everyone knows, the days for mailing out printed cover letters, bios, and resumes are long gone. Electronic communication has streamlined the process, allowing people to convey important information quickly and efficiently. Even though many people don't open attachments, when there is a solid interest, there is often a need for an intact, standalone document that can be easily printed or stored electronically. Here are a few guidelines.

- Make the subject line of your email as provocative, relevant, and on-point as possible. You want to choose a subject that will make them want to open your email. For example, if you are following up on a lead from someone else, make the subject "Referred by Joe Smith", assuming Joe is a good friend or business associate of your recipient. If you know there is an open position, then you could put that in the subject line, such as "Sales Manager Candidate".

- The body of your email is adapted from your cover letter.

- Include a complete "signature" that includes all your contact information. Sometimes it's helpful and appropriate to include your LinkedIn URL.

Chapter 14

YOUR WEB PRESENCE

In the world of job search as well as other professional activities, your web presence will be an important factor for your visibility and success. Anytime someone is curious about you for just about any reason, they will look you up online. In addition, companies use Internet-based social networking sites with increased sophistication to identify, recruit, and vet job candidates. Once a candidate has been identified, the web provides significant intelligence about the person during due diligence.

At a personal level, one of the benefits of these sites is that they allow you to stay in touch with your established network, make new connections and then reinforce those connections. Such tools facilitate people's ability to exponentially expand their networks.

Creating a multi-purpose personal profile communicates what you want the world to know about you. Your professional profile and how you manage your web presence displays your capabilities, essential qualities and personal brand. A good professional headshot is considered essential for most business profile applications.

Currently, the big three social media sites are LinkedIn, Facebook, and Twitter. There are numerous other sites that wax and wane in popularity, such as Instagram,

BEYOND THE BASIC BIO

Pinterest, and Snapchat. Each has a particular audience and purpose. We recommend that you stay informed about how any of these other sites could be important to your profession.

Thanks to the ubiquitous Internet, the details of our lives have become easy to access, and it's getting easier all the time. As such, it is important to understand how these networking sites work and how you can use them to your advantage.

The LinkedIn World: Professional Connections

The King Kong of business social media is **LinkedIn** (linkedin.com). As one of the world's largest social networks, LinkedIn has a half billion members and is still adding 2 new members per second.

> *With [hundreds of millions] of members (mostly professionals in their 30s and older), LinkedIn has become the virtual rolodex for business people.*
> —**Forbes**

It is interesting to note that LinkedIn profiles with photos get 21 times more profile views and 36 times more messages than profiles without photos. This continues to confirm the importance of incorporating a good professional headshot into your profile.

LinkedIn is the go-to site for a wide variety of business applications. It is often the first place recruiters go to find candidates. In fact LinkedIn offers a special service for recruiters searching the LinkedIn database. It is also the cornerstone of good business networking for a job searcher and almost any business connection objective. It is also used by anyone who wants to find out about an individual, for example, before an interview, a business event, or any meeting where someone wants background information about a person.

There are two primary objectives for having a great LinkedIn profile. First, when someone looks you up or finds you in some other way, you want to have an engaging professional presence. Second, you want to be found when someone is looking for a job candidate or a resource of some other kind that you provide.

The best profiles include a targeted headline, compelling summary section that can be derived from your bio, a career history that essentially comes from your resume, and other enhancements such as media, recommendations, affiliations/groups, and credentials. The headline is the most important search field of the profile. If it is not specifically edited, it defaults to your current or most recent position.

Much of your bio goes straight into the summary section of your profile. You can also add bullet points or other information such as areas of expertise or services offered to improve search results and attract more interest. You can also add your bio or other interesting elements as media items in this section.

Professionals who want to maximize their visibility can take advantage of sophisticated approaches to optimizing their LinkedIn page. This is as complicated and dynamic as a Google search optimization process, so it takes time, regular attention and expert help.

The Facebook World: Global Social Networking

Founded by Mark Zuckerberg in 2004 to electronically connect Harvard students, Facebook (FB) is now the leading social networking site in the world. LinkedIn and Facebook may have some similar features, but they have different users and serve different purposes. Facebook users are on average younger than LinkedIn members. And since the younger generation has grown up on Facebook, it is naturally their go-to place.

The site has become a major force for company branding, attracting talent, and candidate vetting. Recruiters are savvy enough to look for younger generation job-seekers on the social network where their targeted candidates hang out. When Facebook users make their pages public, it's a gold mine for recruiters.

BEYOND THE BASIC BIO

No matter what your profile settings are, there is a good chance that you or your postings can be found on the Internet. Accordingly, you should be careful about how you present yourself—it is effectively a public site. For example, the opinions you express on public postings will be visible, and if they are not professionally managed, they can come back to haunt you.

Twitter

Twitter defines itself as "... a service for friends, family, and co-workers to communicate and stay connected through the exchange of quick, frequent messages." It's designed for people to broadcast regular short messages to the world in a quickly scannable format (currently 280 characters)—perfect for our modern attention-deficit world. With substantially more active users than LinkedIn or Facebook, this platform has become a major avenue for businesses to reinforce their brand and engage with their followers. For purposes of this book, there are a few things for you to consider.

Your Twitter account profile is another venue to highlight your brand—upload a professional headshot, include a description and key words that resonate with your targeted message, and create a theme and profile page that shows off your personality. Recruiters not only search on titles, industry, and location but also key words and hashtags. On Twitter, you can search and follow companies or individuals that you want to stay connected with. It's a dynamic platform that allows you to be up to date or conduct research on any topic or person that matters to you professionally (or personally). If you are an active Twitter user or just tweet once in a while, you want to be mindful of what you post and what the professional implications might be. Using it wisely and consistently can produce a positive brand for yourself and strong catnip for potential targets.

Web-based Portfolios

Some people are in a field where a portfolio of achievements or creative samples is mandatory. A personal website is then essential, providing perhaps the only way to present relevant information to a prospective employer, client, supporter, or patron. For example, creative professionals, attorneys, investment bankers, cosmetic surgeons, musicians, artists and journalists need their personal websites to display a broad range of their work by including videos, photos, deal abstracts, article clippings, and audio clips.

Portfolio websites can be very straightforward or more comprehensive, interactive and sophisticated. Stoke your imagination by looking at this website by a graphic designer/artist: www.michellebdesigns.com. To see how a bio can be integrated into this kind of website, go to http://www.michellebdesigns.com/about.

Visibility Issues: Reputation Management

Do you know what is out there about you? What comes up when you "Google" yourself? The Internet and your web presence is a double-edged sword. You need to be visible and need to be found by recruiters, but you also have to be careful that what they find presents you in a favorable light. Internet searches have become a routine part of every employer's sourcing and due diligence process. People have been removed from consideration for a job because of something that pops up in an Internet search. Many people use their Facebook account for sharing primarily social and personal information. They aren't necessarily thinking about their professional presence when they post fun or rowdy pictures. The truth is that this information is often available to employers and recruiters to check you out—and they do.

Our advice is this: Diligently monitor the Internet for what others post about you, and constantly manage your own professional presence on the web—what you say, pictures you post, pages you "like." Others can even create content about you and post it on their sites without your knowing it or giving your permission. This includes anyone from a friend playing a practical joke, an ex-boyfriend/ex-girlfriend, or a disgruntled employee. The damage such inappropriate information ("digital dirt") can do is significant and may be difficult or impossible to overcome.

Chapter 15

PROFILES

An increasingly valuable tool that is being used in both job search and general networking is a Personal Profile. It is more comprehensive than a bio and less detailed than a resume. Essentially, it's a combination of both with the goal of communicating concise, well-targeted information to the reader.

The most common applications of the Personal Profile are:

- Candidates who have important career events over several years that need to be highlighted, for example acquisitions and sales of businesses, landmark legal cases, important crisis management projects, or R&D breakthroughs.

- People who have owned their own businesses or have other non-traditional job experiences, and as a result, a traditional resume may not present them sufficiently.

- Individuals who are seeking opportunities with portfolio companies of private equity firms or other similar roles—it offers a short summary of the most important information that a reader can absorb quickly.

BEYOND THE BASIC BIO

Personal Profiles can be as flexible as you need them to be. Be creative and clearly targeted to your readers, their interests, and their time limitations. Don't fret about the brevity of the Profile—it is common for the reader, if interested, to ask for your Resume or Bio.

Sample Profiles

Included on the following pages are examples of each of these profiles. In creating your own, stay focused on what is important to your reader.

CAREER EVENT PROFILE

JONATHAN BIANCHI

PRESIDENT & CEO
Mid-Cap Healthcare Companies

"Jonathan would bring value as CEO or President in a healthcare business that needs energizing, strategic direction, processes and controls, and operating results."—Healthcare Consulting Partner

Jonathan Bianchi is a business leader who drives companies beyond the status quo to both strategic and actionable solutions that lead to liquidity events. He is a tenacious problem solver who "out thinks" competitors, builds strong board relationships, and engages all stakeholders. As a situational hands-on manager, he attends to the blocking and tackling by setting up processes and accountabilities that drive accomplishments. He is a sought-after mentor who is known for helping people learn to "think their way through problems".

Jonathan holds an MBA in Finance and Economics from Northwest States University and a BA in Sociology from Southwest States College. He currently serves on the Board of an adolescent treatment facility in Chicago, Illinois.

SUCCESSFULLY SOLD 3 COMPANIES
- 3x return on invested capital
- Public and private businesses

TURNED AROUND BUSINESSES
- Identified key issues and specific plans of attack
- Increased revenues and managed cash leading to liquidity events

RAISED OVER $50 MILLION INVESTMENT CAPITAL
- Either as the lead or co-lead

COMPLETED M&A, RESTRUCTURING & REPOSITIONING OF BUSINESSES/ASSETS
- Manufacturing and business integrations
- Product introductions and rationalizations
- Legal and regulatory compliance

LIQUIDITY EVENTS

TechDirect Healthcare—CEO/COO

Led growth over 3 years to $19.5 million revenue and $4.9 million EBITDA profit from $5.6 million revenue and ($2.5 million) EBITDA loss leading to sale of business. Directed overhaul of systems and processes, led optimization programs, and negotiated all contracts. Sold company for $40 million at 12x EBITDA.

NextGen Med (Nasdaq: NGMD)—CEO

Stabilized financial condition of company by managing cash, divesting assets, restructuring and reorganizing business, introducing new service lines, and negotiated or directed merger agreement, HSR, SEC filings, and anti-trust issues associated with sale to NextGen Med. Sold company at 33% premium.

CAX Devices LLC—President

Built sales and profits 320% and 285% respectively in 5 years. Completed acquisition of competitor's products and directed product rationalization, market positioning, manufacturing integration, and capital improvements. Sold business at $1.6x revenue.

555.674.8830 • linkedin.com/in/JonathanBianchi • jbianchi@email.com

BEYOND THE BASIC BIO

SERVICE BUSINESS PROFILE

LEZLIE GARR

PRESIDENT
Certified Professional Resume Writer
Professional Progressions Consulting
ResumeLezlie.com

"Lezlie is polite, professional and FAST! She is easy to work with and asks great questions to guide you through the process."

"I've done resumes in the past with help from others. Lezlie exceeded my expectations. My resume is outstanding."

"Lezlie did an awesome job capturing exactly what I needed to say on my LinkedIn page. She created the vision I was looking for."

As a Certified Professional Resume Writer (CPRW), Lezlie provides personalized assistance with resumes, cover letters, LinkedIn profiles, interview coaching and more. Clients value her keen insight, individualized approach and ability to capture their unique "voice".

Working closely with clients to understand their career goals and exactly what they are looking to accomplish, Lezlie crafts resumes and LinkedIn profiles that convey skills, experience, achievements and potential in a concise, visually pleasing and easily readable format. Also, through personalized one-on-one interview coaching, she provides insight and constructive feedback that help clients build confidence and develop effective interview skills.

Lezlie holds a Bachelor's degree in Integrative Studies: Entrepreneurship and Organizational Leadership from Northern Kentucky University and is pursuing an MBA from Texas A&M University—Corpus Christi.

SERVICES
Don't settle for less than you're worth
We have a proven track record of helping people at all professional levels in a variety of industries achieve their career goals.

TOP NOTCH RESUMES
Personalized to showcase your strongest skills and market your potential

ONE-ON-ONE INTERVIEWING
Focused on building confidence and learning to market yourself effectively

ALL-STAR LINKEDIN PROFILES
Created to gain attention and use LinkedIn's search algorithms to your advantage

FREE INITIAL CONSULTATION
90-DAY GUARANTEE

OUR PROCESS
Get professional, personal attention
You will work by phone and email with Certified Resume Writers, LinkedIn Specialists and experienced Career Consultants.

- Independent research to understand relevant keywords based on job posting
- Complete draft
- Client review and revisions with no set limit (within reason)
- Fully editable MS Word version written with the goal of being successful in online Applicant Tracking Systems (ATS)
- PDF version that displays well on any technology

Time: 7-10 business days with rush service available for resume. 2-4 additional days for LinkedIn profile

Payment: Full payment in advance via PayPal invoice with the option to pay with your PayPal account or with a credit/debit card. Work begins upon notification of payment.

Contact Us
Lezlie@ResumeLezlie.com • 817-476-0683

Reprinted with Permission Professional Progressions Consulting

PROFILES

NON-TRADITIONAL OR UNIQUELY SKILLED PROFILE

STEVEN H. MCDERMOTT

BRAND STRATEGIST
Business Development – Systems Integration

"Steve's commitment to improving the overall quality of the AV industry is obvious. His flexibility and depth of knowledge is why after many decades he is still at the top of the industry." Principal Photographer and Owner, Monarch Photography & Design

"Steve has a vision, one that is forward-thinking and selfless. He sees what needs to be done and does it. He is a breath of fresh air to the industry! Chief Marketing Officer, MSB Systems

Steven H. McDermott has a natural ability to set people at ease and provide a refreshing level of client service. Rarely is there an executive more engaged in creating long-term relationships that establish the foundation for finding solutions and generating a continuing revenue stream.

With a solid character and honest sense of right and wrong developed in childhood, Steve lives his values. It also makes him uniquely qualified for his role as Chair of the AAVP Ethics Committee, which he executes with grace, goodwill, and a sense of humor.

Steve is so well-known in the industry that people simply take his calls and are more willing to buy from him than anyone else. He often works on a handshake and does whatever it takes to get the job done.

RECOGNITIONS & MEDIA COVERAGE
AAVP Lifetime Achievement Award, 2006
AAVP Volunteer of the Year Award, 1999
Keynote Speaker, AVCOM Conference, 2012

Regularly quoted in industry publications including Meetings & Events Magazine, Midwest Technology Review, and Small Business Quarterly

McDERMOTT SOLUTIONS, 1980 – 2014
Nationally recognized audio visual equipment and systems contracting company with key clients ranging from small consumer businesses to large enterprises.

President, CEO and Co-Founder
- Grew the company from the ground up to being recognized in the Alliance of AV Professionals (AAVP) "Top 100" every year since 2008
- Fundamentally changed the business model so manufacturers sold directly to custom integrators, opening a large new market opportunity for manufacturers in the industry
- As a long-term relationship manager, master negotiator, and creator of the "World Famous Southern BBQs" at the AAVP National EXPO, established new bridges between manufacturers and dealers at a pivotal time in the the industry

ALLIANCE of AV PROFESSIONALS, 1989—Present
Leading global authority in the $14 billion audio visual industry with 3,500 member companies serving 22,000 industry professionals.

Board of Directors Member & Ethics Committee Chair
- Leader in giving the industry a voice and providing educational opportunities for the members
- Instrumental in government affairs, including influencing legislation that would have put 1,000 companies out of business in one state alone
- For the past 12 years, led the Ethics Committee in successfully arbitrating and negotiating difficult situations between manufactures and dealers, dealers and clients, and clients and manufacturers

AIR FORCE, Tactical Air Command
Management Analyst
Prepared operational data books, conducted efficiency studies, and briefed Air Force leadership on operational issues

EARLY CAREER
Held sales and general management positions with retail electronics companies

CREDENTIALS
AAVP Certified Instructor
AAVP Certified Outreach Instructors

Western Tech College
Communications Department Advisory Board Chair
Advisory Boards, various industry publications

800.555.9235 • steve@mcdermottsolutions.com • www.McDermottSolutions.com

Chapter 16

BIOS FOR MARKETING

Professional bios are crucial in marketing and sales. As with all bios, these must address the needs of the audience and communicate the objectives of the writer.

Words are important, but they are only part of any marketing package. So take advantage of the opportunity to be graphically creative, making good use of color, pictures and an interesting layout.

If you are an employee with a company whose PR department controls external publications, be sure your bio has been cleared through PR before you distribute it.

Business Proposals

A business proposal requires a special bio, particularly if you are in a consulting or service business. Customers are buying the expertise and problem-solving capabilities of the service team. It is often the most important factor affecting the buying decision. Customers need to be confident that they are purchasing unique skills and specialized knowledge relevant to their challenges. That means that your credentials, experience, and track record need to be presented in a compelling and targeted fashion.

BEYOND THE BASIC BIO

The Business Proposal Bio is most commonly submitted in one of two formats. A text format is usually incorporated into a written proposal, and a bullet format is part of a PowerPoint presentation to the prospective customer.

The **text format** is basically a condensed, shortened version of your Foundation Bio. The key here is to condense the most important statements from your bio into one well-constructed paragraph. Crisply blend together thoughts that may have consumed a full paragraph in your longer bio. This paragraph is more focused on facts and credentials than other formats. If you find that a longer bio is required as part of your business proposal, simply use your Foundation Bio.

The PowerPoint **bullet format** will include 5-6 points, just one or two lines each. Keep the slide short and clean so that it is readable and easy to understand. The slide heading consists of your name and title, on either one line or two. The bullets should provide:

- A short version of the "Who You Are" part of your bio. Select the most important words that describe you.

- Specific expertise or knowledge relevant for the proposal.

- A broad-based statement about your industry, technical, or leadership experience. It could be about the role you have played, years in a particular industry, or a particular position. Since you can also credential yourself by the company you have kept, this is a good place to insert well-recognized names that will impress your audience.

- Special credentials such as relevant certifications, awards, honors, or publications. If appropriate, foreign languages should be mentioned here. While you can use two bullets for this material, the general rule remains "less is more."

- Education

Here is an example of how you might structure your slide bio.

MARCUS SCHWARTZ PRINCIPAL CONSULTANT

- Financial services compliance and risk management consultant
- Experienced in anti-money laundering, foreign assets, fraud prevention, ethics, foreign financial dealings (FCPA), and privacy laws
- Recognized for helping companies reconcile what their lawyers tell them to do and practical approaches to getting it done
- Career with the top tier global financial companies
- Certified Anti-Money Laundering Specialist (CAMS)
- MS in Accounting from New York University

You may need to modify your format to meet the needs of your audience. If this is an internal presentation, for example, you don't need to include your company name. Also, if this is a marketing presentation from your company to a potential customer, the company name is redundant. It's either on the slide, shown in the footer, or obvious somewhere else. If you are making an external presentation where other companies are involved, you will want to include your company name underneath your title.

Finally, if a group of bios are being included in a proposal, they should all be formatted consistently. Hopefully you will have an opportunity to direct or give input on the format of the bios. If you don't, you will want to modify your bio to be consistent with the others.

BEYOND THE BASIC BIO

Websites

Company websites often include the bios of board members, corporate executives, owners, and other key professionals. Large companies also post bios at many levels in the organization on their corporate Intranets. These bios are intended to enhance intra-company communications and cross-functional or cross-organizational visibility, recruiting, and resource management.

Small-to-medium-sized companies are more likely to include bios if they are service businesses. If a small company is selling widgets or generic services (e.g. carpet cleaning), they normally don't need bios. However, if a company is selling professional services, the expertise of its leaders and key staff members is important. Thus, website bio pages should be creative, offering interesting layouts and engaging pictures.

Frequently, websites will display a mini-bio with taglines on a directory-like page with a link or drop-down to the full bio. Some version of your Personal Introduction along with taglines and key words work perfectly here.

Chapter 17

BIOS FOR PUBLIC SPEAKING

Public speakers have to sell themselves as actors and performers—thus, their bios will reflect that. Accordingly, if you are (or desire to be) a public speaker, you should have three basic bios.

- A very short form for inclusion in seminar brochures or marketing flyers

- A somewhat longer podium introduction to be used by the person introducing you

- A more comprehensive bio that is part of the speaker's "one-pager" used for marketing purposes by the agent or other person promoting your appearance

BEYOND THE BASIC BIO

Very Short Form

The seminar brochure may be as short as 50 words—just two to three sentences. It should include your name, title, and company. It should also include the most relevant credential that would bring people to hear you speak on this topic. Here's a good example:

> World-renowned business educator and coach, **Dr. Marshall Goldsmith** is the leading expert in his field. His singular ability to get results for top leaders has drawn over 150 CEOs and their management teams to address change in the workplace. They want what Dr. Goldsmith offers: practical and proven methods.

Podium Introduction

For your speaking engagement, the person who introduces you will appreciate a well-written short introduction that can be read smoothly from the podium. Wouldn't you rather control what they say about you than to take a chance on what someone else might come up with?

It should be 100—150 words that can be read in about **1 minute**. It should be written in simple, easy to read sentences. The best introductions quickly engage the audience and get them jazzed up for the presentation. And it's important for the introduction to validate the speaker's credentials on the topic being presented.

BIOS FOR PUBLIC SPEAKING

> Marshall Goldsmith is one of the world's most accomplished and in-demand executive coaches. His client list is a who's who of the highest level global CEOs. He has helped implement leadership development processes that have impacted more than one million people. His PhD is from UCLA, and he is on the faculty of the executive education programs at Dartmouth College's Tuck School of Business. *Thinkers50* has recognized Marshall as one of the World's Most-Influential Business Thinkers for each of the past ten years. The American Management Association named Marshall one of fifty great thinkers and business leaders who have impacted the field of management. With numerous best-selling books, Amazon.com recognized two of them, *Triggers* and *What Got You Here Won't Get You There*, as being in the Top 100 Leadership and Success Books ever written.

Speaker "One-Pager"

Professional speakers also need a sexy "one-pager" that highlights their range of topics, credentials, and other special selling points. Key information from your Foundation Bio can be incorporated into this document. It is usually a two-sided glossy document much like a marketing flyer. Beyond your experience, credentials, and special expertise for speaking engagements, you will display your speaking topics, testimonials, and pictures. Clever and targeted graphic design can make a big difference. There are lots of sample one pagers on the Internet. Just search for "speaker one pager."

Chapter 18

BIOS FOR PROSPECTIVE BOARD MEMBERS

Many successful executives aspire to sit on Boards of Directors in both the corporate and not-for-profit arenas. These Board positions offer an opportunity to share expertise, gain visibility, and give back to the community. They also provide a great network of high-level contacts and a way to differentiate yourself from your peers. In some cases, these positions offer additional compensation and other benefits.

Boards generally seek people who can make substantive contributions to their organizations. They also favor people who have the standing and stature to make organizations stand out within the community, the industry, or the marketplace.

Expectations will vary from organization to organization. Sometimes Boards are seeking fundraisers. Others seek out people who can provide business advice and counsel. Still others will be looking for diversity or a recognizable brand name. To be a good prospective candidate, it is important to understand your target organization's expectations. You satisfy these requirements and effectively communicate through your bio.

BEYOND THE BASIC BIO

Networking is an essential part of being considered for a board seat. And **bios are the essential tool** for such networking. The bio used for this purpose, however, is somewhat unique. Since Boards are looking for stature and pedigree, it is heavily focused on an individual's **credentials**. A Board member bio must highlight strong credentials that are aligned with the organization. Everything about your background and experience, your customers, your awards, and your degrees needs to be presented with an eye towards credentialing.

In general, Boards are looking for one or more of the following qualities for their Board nominees.

- **Cachet:** Boards want their members to be well recognized so that they can bring an element of stardom and credibility to the company.

- **Functional Expertise:** Boards need to have many business functions represented so that decisions are made with a balanced perspective. The Board is not hiring additional executives to run the business but rather to provide strategic governance.

- **Valuable Relationships:** Board members are expected to be able to open the right doors and access the right resources for their company. They are often selected because they know who to call and can effectively get things done through their networks.

- **Skilled Governance:** A company's strategic policy decisions are made by its Board, with each Board member contributing to the overall governance of the organization. The Board is responsible for bringing thoughtful sophistication to the process of leadership.

BIOS FOR PROSPECTIVE BOARD MEMBERS

For not-for-profit Boards, two additional criteria are applicable.

- **Passion for the Mission:** Not-for-profit Boards want Board members who believe in the organization and can serve as its voice, both formally and informally, internally and externally.

- **Monetary Contributions:** Not-for-profit Boards generally expect their Board members to make material personal monetary contributions in addition to helping the organization raise money from other sources.

The Board Bio

You can craft your new Board Bio directly from your Foundation Bio with an added focus on what the Board needs. Here is additional guidance for developing a compelling Board bio.

Paragraph 1: Positioning Paragraph

Sentence one—Essence Factor: What is your professional essence from the perspective of being a board member? Who are you viewed through the eyes of a board selection committee (and shareholders)? Remember, you may have to be approved by the shareholders. Why would this company want you on their board? What is the most important contribution you think you could make to this particular board? It might be your reputation as a "mover and shaker" within the industry. It might be your track record as a successful entrepreneur.

Sentence two—Guru Factor: What special expertise or unique knowledge can you provide? For example, you might be someone who has a knack for recognizing future technology trends. Or you might be especially astute in emerging legislative or global economic issues.

Sentences three and four—Star Factor: What have you done that has earned you recognition? What particular characteristics make you attractive as a Board candidate? For example, you might be someone who is recognized for your ability to ask profound, provocative questions that guide the decision-making process.

BEYOND THE BASIC BIO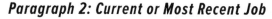

Paragraph 2: Current or Most Recent Job

This paragraph will usually be very similar or the same as the one you wrote for your Foundation Bio. The question to ask yourself is whether the accomplishments that you have highlighted are the same ones you would select to present to the Board Selection Committee. This should showcase strategic leadership as well as governance roles.

Paragraph 3: Prior Experience

This paragraph will likely be very similar or the same as the one you wrote for your Foundation Bio. However, it will be condensed as much as possible and only mention an accomplishment if it is directly relevant for this Board seat. By keeping it short, you leave more room for your credentials.

Paragraph 4: Credentials

Boards like candidates who have already been discovered by other organizations. In other words, if you have been or currently serve as a board member, whether corporate or not-for-profit, then you have an advantage here. List it along with any leadership roles that you have held in industry, civic, or charitable institutions that demonstrate your ability to guide an organization beyond your current or prior positions.

Boards also like people who have been well recognized for their accomplishments, especially with awards or honors from outside their own company. Industry awards, civic honors or honorary degrees are examples of such credentials. Finally, you will want to emphasize any publications, speaking engagements, or other forms of external recognition. Just like in your Foundation Bio, you should include your foreign language skills as well as your degrees and certifications.

Additional Considerations

With notable Board experience, the bio should include a stand-alone paragraph like the one below. Its placement in the bio will depend on how it fits into the overall career progression and other credentials.

BIOS FOR PROSPECTIVE BOARD MEMBERS

Since 2010, Travis has been a member of the Board of Directors of ABC International, where he currently chairs the Nominating Committee, serves on the Compensation Committee, and previously served on the Audit Committee. During his Board tenure, ABC has made a well-managed CEO transition, grown internationally through acquisition, and diversified its portfolio.

For a not-for-profit board, be sure to highlight your passion for the organization's mission and to include information about your ability to bring money into the organization.

Sample Board Bios

A Board Bio will include "Board of Directors Candidate" just under the individual's name. When the person already has Board experience, a list of relevant boards is included in the Heading section. When the person does not have specific Board experience, the candidate should include responsibilities in the bio that reflect such activities as interfacing with Boards or leading governance activities within a functional role, especially in the current or most recent job.

Author Paula Asinof obtained permission from two board-candidate clients to include their bios in *Be Sharp* with their contact information removed. They are presented as they were written at the time of creation, and accordingly their situation is likely different since publication of this book. One of the bios is for a Board of Directors Candidate who already has Board experience. The other is for an individual without prior Board experience.

- **With Board Experience:** Sharon Gabrielson, Chair of Global Business Solutions (Division President Equivalent), Mayo Clinic

- **No Board Experience:** Michele Allegretto, Vice President of Human Resources, Glaukos Corporation

SHARON R. GABRIELSON

Board of Directors Candidate
Current Chair of Global Business Solutions (Division President Equivalent)
Mayo Clinic

Healthcare Solutions
Consumer/Patient-Focused Service Offerings
Provider Organization Leadership

BOARD OF DIRECTORS EXPERIENCE
American Medical Group Association
Mayo Medical Services Inc., a private health plan administrator
Health Traditions Health Plan, a private insurance company
Austin Medical Center, Compensation Chair
Albert Lea Medical Center

SHARON GABRIELSON is dedicated to enhancing the lives of consumers through health and wellness products and services. Recognized for her role in energizing innovative and creative market-driven solutions, she focuses on leveraging portfolio strengths, engaging others in a vision, and taking calculated risks. With the confidence and expertise to make high stakes decisions from research and evidence-based information, Sharon is adept at navigating the changing healthcare environment.

Currently, Sharon is Chair (Division President Equivalent) of the Mayo Clinic's Global Business Solutions Department. She has also served as Administrator of the Clinic's Office of Population Health and Vice Chair of Health System Administration. As Chair of Global Business Solutions, Sharon is transforming an underperforming unit into the heart of Mayo's business diversification and profitability. She directs the domestic and international new business development opportunities for commercializing the Clinic's competencies to deliver service-based products to the B2B and B2C markets. As Vice Chair of Health System Administration, she led a $2 billion revenue generating organization of community-based practices through the transition from "fee for service" to "value-based care". She also led the design and implementation of the new governance structure for Mayo Clinic in the Midwest. In these roles, she was instrumental in developing a strategic plan for market penetration, scaling for growth and competing in a risk-based environment.

Previously at the Mayo Clinic, Sharon rose to a leadership role as Section Head of the Division of Systems and Procedures, the company's management, engineering and internal consulting function. Earlier she held administrative positions with the Olmsted Medical Center and LifeSource Upper Midwest Organ Procurement Organization. She began her career as an RN at Saint Marys Hospital.

Sharon has served on numerous leadership and management committees of Mayo Clinic as well as several industry boards. Her board memberships include American Medical Group Association, Mayo Medical Services, Inc., the Health Tradition Health Plan, the Austin Medical Center as Compensation Committee Chair, and the Albert Lea Medical Center. She has made presentations to industry associations on topics such as competing with disruptive innovators and authored articles with her most recent one being "Developing a new governance structure: the Mayo Clinic Experience". Sharon received an MA in Health Administration and an MA in Management from Saint Mary's University and a BS in Nursing from Winona State University.

BIOS FOR PROSPECTIVE BOARD MEMBERS

MICHELE M. ALLEGRETTO

Board of Directors Candidate
Vice President, Human Resources
Glaukos Corporation

Strategy, Human Capital Management and Structured Governance
Business Alignment
Organizational Effectiveness
Executive Counsel & Thought Leadership
Acquisition Integration

MICHELE ALLEGRETTO is an innovative leader who is passionate that the biggest differentiator of success is a company's talent. Known for impeccable judgement and a forthright yet diplomatic style, she can manage across an organization and influence perspectives. Respected for acquiring in-depth knowledge of the business including its competitive and regulatory landscape, Michele establishes credibility and guides decisions towards outcomes that make sense for the company, its culture and the situation. Above all, she thrives on making a difference in the organization.

Currently, Michele is the Vice President of Human Resources at Glaukos Corporation, a fast-growing international ophthalmic medical technology company focused on breakthrough products to transform the treatment of glaucoma. She serves as a member of the Executive Team where she oversees human resources strategy and operations. She also interfaces with the Board on CEO and senior leadership succession planning, executive compensation, equity awards and related SEC disclosures. In this role, she built a new human resources culture focused on aligning talent management with the business strategy and brought structured human resources governance to the increasingly regulated company.

Previously, Michele joined Abbott Medical Optics as its Director of Global Business Human Resources when it acquired Advanced Medical Optics where she was Director of Human Resources. Among her responsibilities at each company, Michele was the human resources lead on acquisition integration. Earlier, Michele's career spanned three divisions of The Walt Disney Company—Walt Disney Studios, The Disneyland Resort and The Disney Store—focused on a broad range of talent acquisition. When the company opened Disney's *California Adventure, Downtown Disney* and the *Grand Californian* hotel, Michele drove the recruiting strategies and successful executions required to fully staff each property with employees meeting Disney standards. She began her human resources career with a division of The Limited Inc.

Michele received a Bachelor's degree in Psychology and a Master's degree in Industrial and Organizational Psychology from California State University. She has continued her education through various programs on organizational design and effectiveness, change management, and business alignment including a workshop through the University of Michigan's Ross School of Business "Translating Business Strategy: HR's Role in Value Creation". Michele is a member of the National Human Resources Association (NHRA) and the Human Capital Institute.

CONCLUSION

Our goal in writing this book has been to provide you with important tools designed to help you present yourself effectively to others. We have expanded the book with new content to give you additional guidance for applying the methodology more broadly. We have addressed how your introduction can be incorporated into a growing variety of relevant media and diverse opportunities to introduce yourself.

If you follow our methodology, chances are good that you will start to think about yourself differently. The process of crafting an introduction and creating a bio requires you to explore and articulate your most important talents and accomplishments. It is a remarkably effective way to focus on the positive and clarify your messages. We are confident that the person you discover while going through that process will be stronger, better defined, and more dynamic than you realized.

So take the time to explore the process. Give it a try. Practice it over and over and over—not until you get it right, but until you can't get it wrong. It needs to be a natural part of you. The next time you are asked to introduce yourself, you will be able to answer with confidence, poise, and panache.

You never get a second chance to make a first impression.
—**Will Rogers**

ABOUT THE AUTHORS

Paula Asinof
Principal & Founder
Yellow Brick Path
yellowbrickpath.com

Paula Asinof is the founder of Yellow Brick Path, a career coaching, consulting, and resume services firm. She also advises Board of Directors candidates on their bios. Her firm was recognized as the Best Career Coaching Firm in Texas by US Business News. Clients appreciate her straight talk, often unconventional perspectives, and the depth of her "real world" executive experience. Paula's background includes Executive Search recruiting and leadership positions in IT and Finance with GTE (now Verizon), Rand McNally, and the Chicago Stock Exchange. She began her career in public accounting. Paula holds an MBA from The Wharton School, an MA from Columbia University, and a BA from Washington University in St. Louis. She is an Associate of Career Thought Leaders, a Member of the International Coach Federation (ICF), and Certified NLP Coach.

Mina Brown
Founder & President
Positive Coach LLC
positivecoach.com

Mina Brown is an experienced and masterful executive coach, career consultant, author, trainer, and public speaker. She provides individual and enterprise-wide executive coaching, and her Coach Academy International provides ICF-accredited coach training. Her clients come from a broad spectrum of industries such as technology, aerospace, financial services, manufacturing, and real estate. Previously, Mina was CFO of Aviall, Inc. and also SVP/GM of its Aerospace Division. Earlier she was in management with Ryder System and Amax. She started her career with Price Waterhouse. She is an ICF Master Certified Coach (MCC), Board Certified Coach, Certified Hogan Coach, and Master NLP Practitioner. Mina holds an MBA from Vanderbilt University and a BBA from Eastern Kentucky University. A popular keynote speaker and workshop facilitator, she is also a certified MBA/EMBA Coach for Vanderbilt's Owen Graduate School of Management.

ABOUT THE AUTHORS

CHECK OUT THE AUTHORS' OTHER POPULAR BOOKS

Be Smart: Sail Past the Hazards of Conventional Career Advice

Everything you've been doing could be wrong! The world of job search and career management has evolved radically in the past ten years. This collection of substantive yet entertaining essays challenges assumptions and shakes the trees of "conventional wisdom." The authors have written this book to provide straightforward advice that is simple, intuitive, and easy to apply. They have helped hundreds of clients unravel all sorts of "messes" that have resulted from bad advice, much from seemingly expert sources. They know how hiring is done, what can get someone in trouble, and what really works. Consider how career management and job search are like sailing. Successful careers are about strategy, competition, and determination. Careers rarely move in a straight line and are unpredictable. Yet, the exhilaration of the race can be satisfying and rewarding. This book will help you sail on with gusto and navigate the ups and downs that come with the journey!

Making Practical Sense of Career Management: A Comprehensive Guide for Modern Career Coaching

A detailed workbook designed to support career management coaches and other professionals. In today's coaching environment, professional coaching frequently involves career coaching. Often coaching engagements, especially in the business or executive arena, include helping clients figure out what to do with their careers, how to advance in a company, and how to conduct a job search. Career coaching is a lucrative business and relatively insulated from economic cycles. Most "career coaching" is not "pure coaching"—it involves a blending of "knowing" (expertise, training) and "not knowing" (coaching). Career Coaches move in and out of these roles to meet their clients' needs. They are at various times consultants, trainers, mentors, or coaches. This self-study workbook emphasizes the importance of coaching—questioning, challenging, and letting the client lead throughout career management and job search engagements. Whether you are new to career coaching, already conduct career coaching, or want to add it as a specialty to your current business, this workbook is invaluable.

Made in the USA
Columbia, SC
03 September 2018